TRUE CRIME KILLERS

VOLUME 3

Ben Oakley

SELECT TITLES BY BEN OAKLEY

FICTION

HARRISON LAKE INVESTIGATIONS
The Camden Killer
The Limehouse Hotel
Monster of the Algarve

HONEYSUCKLE GOODWILLIES
The Mystery of Grimlow Forest
The Mystery of Crowstones Island

SUBNET SF TRILOGY
Unknown Origin
Alien Network
Final Contact

NONFICTION

TRUE CRIME
Bizarre True Crime Series
Monsters of True Crime Series
True Crime Killers Series
Orrible British True Crime Series
The Monstrous Book of Serial Killers
Year of the Serial Killer

OTHER NONFICTION
The Immortal Hour: The True Story of Netta Fornario
Suicide Prevention Handbook

As a thank you for adding this book to your collection, we would like to offer you a FREE eBook for simply signing up to our mailing list. Along with a free book, you'll get weekly updates from the world of true crime brought to you by truecrimelists.com, and early book release notifications so you can be the first to get them at an introductory price, exclusively for subscribers.

Visit WWW.TRUECRIMELISTS.COM and click on FREE BOOK from the menu.

Copyright © 2023 Ben Oakley.

First published in 2023 by Twelvetrees Camden.

This edition 2023.

The right of Ben Oakley to be identified as the
Author of the Work has been asserted by him in accordance
with the Copyright, Designs and Patents Act 1988.

Visit the author's website at www.writetheplanet.co.uk

All rights reserved. No part of this book may be reproduced, or stored in a retrieval system, or transmitted in any form or by any means, electronic, mechanical, photocopying, recording, or otherwise, without express written permission of the publisher.

Each case has been fully researched and fact-checked to bring you the best stories possible and all information is correct at the time of publication. This book is meant for entertainment and informational purposes only.

While the publisher and author have used their best efforts in preparing this book, they make no representations or warranties with respect to the accuracy or completeness of the contents of this book. Neither the publisher nor the author shall be liable for any loss of profit or any other commercial damages, including but not limited to special, incidental, consequential, personal, or other damages.

The author or publisher cannot be held responsible for any errors or misinterpretation of the facts detailed within. The book is not intended to hurt or defame individuals or companies involved.

ISBN: 978-1-915929-15-0

Cover design by Ben Oakley. Images by Marina Luisa.

For information about special discounts available
for bulk purchases, sales promotions, book signings,
trade shows, and distribution, contact
hello@twelvetreescamden.co.uk

Twelvetrees Camden Ltd
71-75 Shelton Street, Covent Garden
London, WC2H 9JQ

www.twelvetreescamden.co.uk

True Crime Killers Volume 3

Bloody Benders 15

The World's End Murderer 27

Templeton Woods Killer 37

The Other Bathory 49

The Beenham Child Killer 59

The Black Panther 71

Body in the Garden 85

The West's 95

The Shoe Fetish Slayer 107

Killer in the Casino 117

Babes in the Ditch Murderer 125

A Victorian Murder 139

Thames Torso Murders 149

Axeman of New Orleans 159

The Norfolk Woods Butcher 169

Maniac Cop 177

Babes in the Wood 1986 185

Murder of Marvin Gaye 197

18 real-life stories of serial killers and murderers with solved and unsolved killings from the USA, UK, Europe, and beyond.

Thank you very much for choosing this book for your collection! The true crime community is one I've fallen in love with over the years and I'm truly grateful for your support. To readers new and old, I raise my glass to you. In fact, it's down to my readers that this new series exists at all.

The mission behind TRUE CRIME KILLERS is as simple as it sounds, to share with you stories of real-life murders and the killers behind them. The cases are laid out in a concise, easy to read format, with all the facts and information you need. If you want a 300-page read on each case, this is not that book.

This is a true crime anthology series with 18 stories in each volume. Inside each volume you'll discover serial killers and murderers with solved and unsolved killings from the USA, UK, Europe, and beyond. Some you know, some you don't.

Many of the other series' released through Twelvetrees Camden are general true crime anthology books. They include the whole gamut, from murders to robberies and frauds to cybercrime. But TRUE CRIME KILLERS has one focus – murder.

Which needless to say means some of the stories contain descriptions of such an act. Where other books go all in on the gore, there is some restraint shown here – as much as is possible. But this is not a book about fluffy rabbits, it's a book about humans killing other humans, so expect a little darkness to come your way.

Let's take a journey through the history of murder from the UK to the USA and discover the first family of serial killers, tale of the other Bathory, child killers, case of the Black Panther, a body in the garden, dark fetishes, killer in the casino, Victorian mysteries, a maniac cop, an unusual axeman, serial killers, and other real-life horror stories.

First, a warning.

Due to the nature of this book and the subject it discusses, there are depictions of murder included in some of the stories. **This is from the outset of this book.** If you know what you are getting yourself into and know what real-life killers likely do, then let us proceed.

Here are previews of the 18 real-life true crime stories within these blackened pages.

Bloody Benders

The first family of serial killers ran a guesthouse to snare their victims with a secret trap door, until one day they vanished, leaving behind a tale of folklore, conspiracies, and macabre discoveries.

The World's End Murderer

Angus Sinclair was a dangerous predator capable of sinking to the depths of depravity, convicted of four murders and linked to many more, he was one of Britain's worst serial killers.

Templeton Woods Killer

After the first Templeton Woods murder, girls stopped walking the streets alone, after the second, the area became ground zero for Britain's most infamous cold case, with links to the Zodiac Killer.

The Other Bathory

One of history's worst female murderers had a hobby of torturing and killing slaves, but escaped justice due to her wealth and connections, before becoming revered in Chilean culture.

The Beenham Child Killer

A child killer claimed two young lives, shocking a small Berkshire village, but the killer was a local who had already claimed another victim six months earlier, and would escape justice for 45 years.

The Black Panther

With over 400 thefts, 19 post office robberies, four murders, and countless assaults to his name, the Black Panther was Britain's most prolific criminal, known for the disturbing death of a kidnapped girl.

Body in the Garden

A ten-year-old girl was abducted and murdered in Notting Hill, leading to a 100-year-old cold case, which despite a strong suspect and solid investigatory work, remains officially unsolved to this day.

The West's

A cruel tale of serial killing, abuse, and Britain's most evil couple, Fred and Rose West, who buried the bodies of their victims under the patio in their garden.

The Shoe Fetish Slayer

The dark tale of a killer, whose overpowering fetish for women's shoes, led him to abduct and murder his victims while dressed as a woman – before committing unspeakable acts against their corpses.

Killer in the Casino

A teenager killed a young girl in a casino restroom and pushed her body into the toilet, minutes after his friend walked in on the attack – and did nothing.

Babes in the Ditch Murderer

Raymond Morris, known as the A34 Killer, Babes in the Ditch murderer, or Monster of Cannock Chase, killed three girls and abused many more, leading to one of the largest manhunts in British history.

A Victorian Murder

In Victorian London, a lady of the night was found in her room with her throat slashed, and the door locked from the outside. Read the story of one of the oldest unsolved murders in London.

Thames Torso Murders

In Victorian London, the dismembered bodies of eight women turned up across the city, during the same period when Jack the Ripper was active.

Axeman of New Orleans

A mystery serial killer with a penchant for axes and bloody murder, threatened to kill more people on a specific date – unless he heard jazz music echoing throughout the city.

The Norfolk Woods Butcher

In the Norfolk woods, a man was found butchered to death, believed to have been mauled by a wild beast, but he was the victim of a former Marine with a hatred for dog walkers.

Maniac Cop

In one of modern times most eerie unsolved cold cases, a fitness instructor was killed in a local church by a person dressed in police SWAT gear.

Babes in the Wood 1986

Two nine-year-old girls were lured to their deaths by a monster who escaped justice for 32 years due to errors in the way forensics handled the original evidence.

Murder of Marvin Gaye

Marvin Gaye helped shape Motown in the 1960s and went on to become one of the most influential American artists of all time – who was shot dead by his own cross-dressing preacher father.

Bloody Benders

The first family of serial killers ran a guesthouse to snare their victims with a secret trap door, until one day they vanished, leaving behind a tale of folklore, conspiracies, and macabre discoveries.

In the winter of 1870, a family of four arrived by wagon to the frontier prairie lands of Labette County, Kansas. They called themselves the Bender family, consisting of John Bender, his wife Elvira, and their two children, John Jr. and Kate, said to be of Germanic origin.

The family were already well-off enough to have registered over 160 acres of land in the county. They built a multipurpose cabin that included a storefront where they sold goods to locals and travellers, and an inn above their own living quarters, all strategically placed next to the long and winding Osage Trail.

It was to provide relief to frontier travellers heading through the last days of the Wild West. They also opened up their dining room for travellers wishing to stop for a hot meal, combining multiple businesses into one dwelling.

Elvira and Kate created a two-acre vegetable patch and apple orchard close to the cabin, the fruits of which they sold in the family shop, and to create special meals for their guests – sometimes their last suppers.

The family were unusual because of their belief in spiritualism and their claim to neighbours that they could communicate with the dead. By 1873, the Benders had murdered at least 11 people using an elaborate trapdoor built into the foundations of the cabin.

South Kansas in the 19th Century was a bloody place with territory battles, attacks by Indians, and Civil War fallout. Many pioneers headed to the trails in Kansas and fought for the right to own part of the land.

After the bulk of the Civil War ended in 1865, the U.S. Government moved the native Osage Indians out of Labette County to a new territory, that would later become known as Oklahoma. The land the Indians were forced from was put up for sale to thousands of homesteaders and farmers.

One of these families were the Benders, who appeared to work hard to earn their living like other pioneers in the region. When they arrived, John was 60, and Elvira, 55. John was said to have been an intimidating presence, standing over six feet, with deep-set black eyes, giving him the nickname of 'old beetle-browed John'.

Elvira, who couldn't speak much English, was referred to as the 'she-devil' due to her unfriendliness and disregard of travellers and locals. It was suspected she had her origins in Germany but later researchers point to her origin being Scandinavian.

John Jr. and Kate were in their mid-twenties, were considered handsome, and spoke English with an upper-class accent, not common in the area at the time. Kate claimed to be a psychic healer and would offer her services at the Bender cabin, becoming one of the main draws for travellers.

It was known to be John Jr. and Kate who were the faces of the business, with the other two remaining mostly behind the scenes due to them being disliked by the community. So disliked in fact that Elvira was also known as a midnight hag with the soul of a grave-robbing hyena.

From 1871, many travellers would stop for a meal or to stock up on supplies for the trip out West through Labette County. Many of these were carrying large sums of money due to buying land, stock, or a claim on a section of land being auctioned by the state.

Due to the violence of the times, it was not uncommon for people to go missing in the wildlands, which certainly prolonged the Bender's time at the killing machine they had built. Some family members of the missing people traced their loved ones to the cabin but nothing beyond, and yet suspicions fell, not on the Bender's, but of rogue Indians to the west or horse thieves and general villainy.

In May of 1871, the body of a man called Jones was found in Drum Creek, not too far from where the Bender's cabin sat. Within a few months, two more bodies were discovered nearby. All three men exhibited the same wounds, having had their skulls crushed and throat's cut.

In 1872, George Lochner and his daughter were passing through Kansas to Iowa to visit family. When they didn't make it to Iowa, the alarm bells were sounded, as George was known to be carrying a substantial amount of cash.

George was well-known and had many friends, including Dr. William York, who was a neighbour of his. When York heard they hadn't arrived in

Iowa, he took it upon himself to find out what had happened but he too disappeared somewhere in Labette County.

When York went missing, his brothers formed a search party. One of his brother's was Colonel Alexander York, a Civil War veteran, lawyer, and member of the Kansas State Senate. He organised a 50-strong search party to scour the route that his brother had taken.

In March 1873, the Colonel and his party arrived at the Bender cabin, having traced his brother through Kansas. The Bender's claimed that York had indeed stayed with them but that he had travelled west after only one night.

The colonel was convinced he was being told the truth and was persuaded by Kate to stay for dinner. The Bender's then cooked dinner for the entire search party and suggested that Indians were most likely to blame for York's disappearance.

Five days later, the Colonel returned to the cabin after he had been told a story of a woman who had escaped the inn after being threatened with a knife by Elvira. Due to her lack of English, John Jr. and Kate dismissed the claims as folly but Elvira shouted out that the woman who accused her was actually a witch who deserved to be hanged.

The Colonel and his party left the cabin but were convinced the family had something to do with his brother's death. The Colonel spread the word to neighbouring communities that something was amiss and secrets were being kept by someone in the Osage community.

At around the same time, reports of people going missing on the trail were so common that travellers began avoiding the area altogether. This led the Osage community to call a meeting to find out what was going on.

Around 80 people made up of locals and business owners turned up to the Harmony Grove Schoolhouse for the meeting, including both John's. The meeting concluded that a search warrant would be obtained for every homestead and property from Big Hill Creek to Drum Creek, including the Bender's cabin.

A few days after the meeting, a farmer was passing the Bender cabin when he noticed that the cattle were unfed, and the farm appeared to be abandoned. Another week passed before a search party turned up at the cabin, with Colonel York in tow. When they entered the cabin, the Bender's were nowhere to be seen. They had vanished without a trace.

There was a smell of death coming from every part of the cabin. They found a trap door in the floor of the cabin that had been nailed shut. When they opened it, the smell got worse. The team of mostly men, managed to lift the entire cabin off the ground and move it to the side so they could dig underneath it.

They found clotted blood mixed in with the soil but no bodies. They used metal rods to push into the ground around the cabin, and within an hour, they found the body of William York in a shallow grave in the vegetable patch.

Working through the night and into the morning, the team found another nine grave sites, eight bodies in the mud, and one in the cabin's well. They also unearthed various body parts. All the victims had their skulls crushed with a hammer and their throats cut, apart from a young girl who had been strangled to death.

The site where the bodies were found was given the damning name of 'Hell's Half-Acre'. A newspaper report at the time reported that the search team was so angry they had hung a local man known to the Benders from a beam in the inn. They then resuscitated him and hung him again before letting him go, when they realised he knew nothing.

When stories of the murders reached every corner of the country, thousands of people flocked to the site, from as far afield as New York. Investigators at the time deduced that the Benders had a plan in place for each of their victims.

Each victim was a guest who was beckoned to sit at the dining table in a specific position that was above the trapdoor. The seat was in front of a curtain that separated two rooms. With the victim's back to the curtain, Kate would distract them with tales of spirituality.

One of the men then quietly pulled back the curtain and smashed the victim over the head with a hammer, before cutting their throat. The trap door was activated with a lever and the body would drop down into the cellar. They would rob the victims of all their possessions.

The victims were then either buried whole or dissected. Though some of the victims were well-off and were carrying large amounts of cash with them, others were not, and yet the Bender's had still killed them.

It was concluded at the time that the Bender's had killed for the thrill of killing but other researchers have claimed that they were performing human sacrifices at the whim of Kate, who may or may not have been a witch herself.

Stories emerged of neighbours being threatened with knifes, John Sr. walking around with a large hammer, and blood stains on the family's wagon. Many of the stories that came after the Bender's left were considered to be only speculation.

A lot of effort was put into tracking down the Bender's. The wagon and its malnourished horses were found abandoned 12 miles away near the railroad city of Thayer. As the bender's had left over a week before the search party came knocking, no-one would have been looking for them as they caught a train out of Thayer.

Detectives traced their train journeys. The family had bought tickets to Humboldt, 22 miles away, but John Jr. and Kate left halfway through the journey at Chanute. From there, they caught a train to Texas towards an outlaw colony between Texas and New Mexico, where no lawmen dared tread as none had returned alive.

John Sr. and Elvira continued on the train to Kansas City and bought tickets for the next train to St. Louis, Missouri. From then, what happened to the Bender's remains confined to the pages of folklore as they had vanished from the face of the earth.

One story suggested that the family had been caught by a group of vigilantes, who burned Kate alive and shot dead the other three, assuming Kate to have been a witch. Another group claimed to have hung them and thrown their bodies in a river. But no-one ever claimed the substantial reward.

Stories have been told over time that claimed John Sr. was in fact an immigrant named John Flickinger, but no solid evidence has ever proved it. A man was arrested in Idaho the following year after killing a man with a hammer but he was never proven to be connected to the Bender murders.

Many people were arrested who were thought to be associated with the Bender's but no link was proven. Despite claims that various people were in fact the Bender's, no trace of them was every truly found.

They had simply arrived in Kansas, cash-in-hand, and built a cabin with a trap door purely to ensnare and kill people, and it's that aspect that haunts people a century-and-a-half later. They knew before they built the cabin they were going to kill.

Modern day interpretations of the story suggest the Bender's had killed before and moved to Kansas to set up a new death site. Bones found at the site suggested that the family had killed at least 24 people, more than the official 11 they are linked with.

The cabin was destroyed within days by souvenir hunters who took everything, including the wood of the trap door and the stones from the cellar wall. Some of the pieces of the cabin, including the hammer used in the murders were put on display in a museum in 1967.

No-one truly knows who the Bender's were or where they ended up. Their motives remain confined to the history books. Maybe, descendants of the Bender's live on to this day, unaware of their grim heritage, or maybe they were caught by vigilantes and killed.

The land would forever be known as Hell's half-acre and is said to be haunted. The little slaughterhouse on the prairie and the story of the bloody Bender's continues to fascinate and intrigue to this day.

The World's End Murderer

Angus Sinclair was a dangerous predator capable of sinking to the depths of depravity, convicted of four murders and linked to many more, he was one of Britain's worst serial killers.

On 20th November 1978, the body of 17-year-old Mary Gallacher was found on waste ground near a footbridge at Barnhill Railway Station, in Glasgow, Scotland. She would come to be known as a victim of one of Britain's worst serial killers but it took another 23 years to bring the killer to justice.

The judge who first sentenced Angus Sinclair told him he was '*a dangerous predator capable of sinking to the depths of depravity.*' No truer words were spoken about the man who would become known as The World's End Murderer.

In 1961 at the age of just 16, Sinclair killed his seven-year-old neighbour Catherine Reehill. She was visiting family in Glasgow's Woodlands when she went to a nearby shop only to never return. Sinclair lured her to his family home where he raped and strangled her to death.

Even at such a young age, his callousness was well known. After killing Catherine, he threw her body down the stairs then called an ambulance and claimed she had fallen in an accident. The police saw right through his evil ways and arrested him for murder.

Unfortunately for his future victims, he was able to strike a plea deal where he was sentenced to a lesser charge of culpable homicide. He was released six years into a ten year sentence and was allowed to kill again – and again.

World's End

Upon his release, in his early twenties, he got married and had a son, nothing was seemingly untoward for a short while. On 15th October 1977, two teenagers named Helen Scott and Christine Eadie were seen leaving the World's End Pub on Edinburgh's Royal Mile.

The next day, Christine's naked body was discovered by hikers in East Lothian. Helens' body was found over six miles away in a corn field. They had been raped, abused, beaten, and strangled to death with their bodies left in the open without any attempt to hide them.

The murders of Helen and Christine would later become known as the World's End Murders, and Sinclair; The World's End Murderer. Due to the media running with the story in a big way, some witnesses suggested they had seen the girls with two men that night.

This claim was backed up by police who said that both girls had been tied with different knotting methods. As a possible link between two men was made, the investigation garnered widespread attention and over 13,000 witness statements were taken.

500 suspects were drawn up but no culprit was identified at the time. At the time of the World's End murders, the police had failed to make a connection with four other women who had been found and killed in a similar fashion throughout the same year.

Murder spree

A cold case investigation discovered that during 1977, six young women had disappeared after nights out across the central belt of Scotland, which is generally referred to as a fifty mile stretch from Glasgow to Edinburgh.

Along with Helen and Christine, four other victims were later linked to Sinclair. 37-year-old Frances Barker disappeared outside her home in Maryhill in July 1977 after getting a taxi home from visiting family in Parkhead.

When her body was found at a waste ground, 44-year-old sex offender Thomas Young was arrested and convicted of her murder. At every step of the way, he protested his innocence, and it wouldn't be until his death in prison in 2014 that Sinclair was linked to Barker's murder.

20-year-old Glasgow brewery worker Anna Kenny disappeared in August 1977 after leaving the Hurdy Gurdy bar in the city. She was raped and strangled, and her decomposed remains were found two years later in Skipness, Argyll.

In October 1977, 36-year-old Hilda McAuley was raped, beaten and found dumped on wasteland in Langbank, Renfrewshire. In December, 23-year-old Agnes Cooney disappeared after a night out at the Clada social club in Govanhill. She was tortured, stabbed 26 times and dumped on moorland at Caldercruik. Sinclair was later linked to all four murders but justice was decades away.

Escaping justice

In May of 1978, the investigation was scaled down. The World's End murders, at least for a while, fell into dark Scottish legend. As the investigation dwindled, Sinclair saw opportunity to kill again. His inability to control his urges would lead to the 1978 killing of 17-year-old Mary Gallacher on a footpath in Glasgow.

She was abducted under cover of darkness, raped and strangled to death with a ligature made from the leg of her trousers before her throat was cut for good measure. She was found dead on a dumping ground, nude from the waist down, exposed to the elements.

Sinclair would not be convicted of that particular murder until 2001, when DNA matching cold cases connected him to the crime. It had remained until then, one of Scotland's most mysterious murders.

The Gallacher murder deepened the divide between Glasgow and Edinburgh as the investigation into her death was not as large as the two Edinburgh murders the year before. It was assumed by some that murders in Glasgow were not deemed as important as those in Edinburgh, due to the poverty and cultural divide between Scotland's two largest cities.

Gallacher's murder led Sinclair to change the way he chose his victims. There had been a witness to her abduction and the police were closing in, albeit to the wrong people but Sinclair turned his attention elsewhere.

Psychologists believed it was the witness that led Sinclair to devise different tactics. Unfortunately, it led him to start preying on children. Between 1978 to 1982, Sinclair raped, sexually abused, or assaulted dozens of young girls in the Glasgow area.

He was arrested in 1982 and pleaded guilty to the rape and sexual assault of 11 girls between the ages of six to 14-years-old. He was sentenced to life in prison for the abuse but it was almost 20 years later that he would be charged with murder.

Operation Trinity

A 2000 cold case review of Mary Gallacher's murder linked Sinclair's DNA to her death, leading to his conviction of her murder in 2001, 23 years later, and getting him another life sentence. In 2004, realising Sinclair may have murdered more, three Scottish police forces came together and formed Operation Trinity, to review all the 1977 murders and hundreds of others before and after.

Forensic experts proved that the other four murders of 1977 showed they had a unique signature belonging to Sinclair. Incidentally, Sinclair had provided his DNA voluntarily while in prison.

It was also claimed he carried out some of the murders with his brother-in-law Gordon Hamilton who died in 1996 before justice could find him. Recent evidence showed that Hamilton was implicit in at least one of the murders.

By 2007, the World's End murders had been attributed to him but the trial was to collapse in an extraordinary miscarriage of justice. Sinclair's lawyers had put forward two special defences, one that included the belief the two girls had consented to sexual intercourse with Sinclair.

The second being that anything that happened after that – the murders – were the actions of Gordon Hamilton. Because there was insufficient evidence to prove any sexual encounter had not been consensual then the judge infamously dismissed the case.

Double jeopardy

The news of the verdict caused mass outcry in Scotland and widespread criticism of the police and justice system. The resulting shift in Scottish Law was felt internationally as the Scottish Parliament managed to legally circumnavigate the double jeopardy law.

It was a law which used to mean that one couldn't be tried for the same crime twice. But in 2011, the Scottish Parliament passed the Double Jeopardy Act 2011. It had made various provisions for circumstances when a person convicted or acquitted of an offence could be newly prosecuted.

As such, in 2014, there was a controversial retrial of the World's End murders, which involved the jury visiting the locations where the bodies were found. Sinclair was then found guilty of Helen and Christine's murders in November 2014.

He was sentenced to life in prison on top of his convictions for abuse and the murder of Mary Gallacher. Sinclair was the first person in Scotland to be given a retrial of the same crimes under the new law. His parole date would have been when he was 108-years-old, meaning he was never going to be released from prison.

Sinclair died of natural causes in HM Prison Glen Ochil on 11th March 2019. He was never charged with the four additional murders of 1977 but they have since been linked to him through DNA evidence and cold case reviews. He killed at least seven people and abused at least 11 more but he had left behind many more deaths in his wake.

The family of Hilda McAuley suffered from a suicide relating to the case. Anna Kenny's parents died young, as did her brother, supposedly due to the stress of losing a family member. Other family members of the dead still hold a grudge against a police investigation they say failed them.

Angus Sinclair was one of Britain's most notorious serial killers, with additional murders linked to him using modern research techniques. Gordon Hamilton, it seemed, managed to get away with murder, but if they had worked together as a pair, it seems certain there are many more victims out there.

Ultimately, for the families of the dead, the monster who took their loved ones is long gone, confined to the corridors of hell for eternity.

Templeton Woods Killer

After the first Templeton Woods murder, girls stopped walking the streets alone, after the second, the area became ground zero for Britain's most infamous cold case, with links to the Zodiac Killer.

Located a short drive north of Dundee City Centre, in Scotland, Templeton Woods is considered a great place to visit for walking, cycling, horse riding, picnics, or to watch the wonderful wildlife that lives there. You might even spot a red squirrel or two!

Templeton Woods is a relatively small council wood, covering an area of just under 150 acres, dwarfed by some of Scotland's larger landscapes. Surprising then that the woods are known across the world, not as a place of beauty, but of murder.

From 1979 to 1987, three murders of young women took place in and near the woods, and although one of them appeared to be solved, the other two remain a mystery to this day.

Combined with reports of women being attacked there as recently as 2017, then perhaps it's no surprise why Templeton Woods is draped in such infamy and terror.

1979

As a schoolgirl, Carol Lannen didn't leave much of an impression on her peers at the time, she was a quiet girl who kept herself to herself and didn't have many friends to shout about. However, her death at the age of 18, did leave an impression.

On 21st March 1979, prostitute Carol got into a red estate car on Exchange Street in Dundee City and it was the last time anyone saw her alive – apart from her killer. The next day, her nude body was found near a picnic table in Templeton Woods. She had been tied up and strangled to death.

As the police investigation grew, other prostitutes were able to describe the driver of the red car to police. Over 6,000 owners of red cars were interviewed and an artist-sketch of the suspect, based on the witness accounts, was released to the public.

11 days later, her personal belongings and clothes were found on the side of River Don, over 70 miles away, north of Aberdeen. The murder of Carol Lannen changed the way teenage girls in Dundee conducted themselves, according to recent interviews of women who were teenagers at the time.

And like many crimes in the 1970s, the case went cold and the murder went unsolved, a dark footnote to cap off a year of change for the country. Until 1980, when a second murder in Templeton Woods rocked Dundee and the whole of Scotland.

1980

As a trainee nursery nurse, 20-year-old Elizabeth McCabe needed to let her hair down occasionally. In February 1980, she and a friend went out drinking in popular bars around Dundee. She left a nightclub in the early hours of 11th February – and never made it home.

She was reported missing by her family the same morning. Two weeks later, on the day of what would have been her 21st Birthday, Elizabeth's body was found by two rabbit hunters out walking their dogs, who initially thought they had unearthed a mannequin.

When police arrived, they found her partially nude body in the undergrowth. She had been strangled to death, just 150 metres away from where Carol's body was discovered 11 months earlier. When the newspapers got hold of it and linked it to the 1979 death, the *Templeton Woods Murders* were birthed into existence.

With the severe possibility that a serial attacker was loose in Dundee, the police launched what would become the largest murder investigation the region had ever seen. An estimated 7,500 people were interviewed, and the records of every accommodation owner in the city were scoured for clues.

But as in the death of Carol Lannen, the case went cold – until 2005. Using new forensic techniques, former taxi driver Vincent Simpson was arrested and charged with Elizabeth's murder, based on the evidence that his DNA was found on a blue jumper near the body – which may or may not have had anything to do with the murder.

Unsurprisingly, after a seven-week trial, the jury found Simpson not guilty. The police admitted the evidence had been fundamentally flawed and potentially contaminated. However, the police were known to have fixated their efforts on taxi drivers in the city to such an extent that they took manpower away from other possibilities.

And so it was that Elizabeth McCabe's murder fell into the realm of the unsolved the same way Carol's had. But in 1987, a murder in nearby Melville Lower Wood, led to an altogether different suspect.

1987

30-year-old Lynda Hunter worked with the Samaritans and was a qualified social worker who disappeared on 21st August 1987. The next day, her husband, Andrew Hunter, officially reported her missing.

Immediately, due to his suspicious nature, Andrew became the suspect in her disappearance but the police needed more evidence – or a body – to charge him with anything. They began investigating his life and pulling the pieces apart.

Andrew was a voluntary worker at the Salvation Army, where he had met Lynda via the Samaritans, and they had an affair while he was still married. In December 1984, his wife, Christine, died of suicide, found hanging by a noose in the attic of her home.

During his relationship with Lynda, he took a gay lover and visited gay saunas in Glasgow and Edinburgh. He was also known to every prostitute in Dundee, becoming a regular client to many, and to top it off, he had a 22-year-old drug addicted girlfriend on the side.

Seven months after her disappearance, Lynda's body was found in Melville Lower Wood, in Ladybank, Fife, just 18 miles from Templeton Woods. She had been strangled with her dog lead. Police swooped in on Andrew Hunter and arrested him for her murder.

Despite pleading his innocence, Andrew was charged and ultimately convicted of Lynda's murder in 1988. Andrew had killed her because she became pregnant and he dumped her body in the woods to hide the evidence. Just five years later, in 1993, Andrew died of a heart attack while in prison. But some suggest he had taken many secrets to the grave.

Enter the sleuths

Hunter's case had gained considerable interest across the entire United Kingdom, as it was the first Scottish case to be shown on the national Crimewatch program in 1987. Because of that, Andrew was linked to the Templeton Woods murders, not least because of his regular visits to Dundee.

The description of the driver given to police by witnesses in the Carol Lannen case seemed to be a strikingly close fit to that of Hunter. He was also known to have abused his wife, and Lynda, along with having a penchant for walks through local woods and fetishized sex.

While many have linked him with the Templeton Woods murders, he never gave any inclination he was involved, and any supposed evidence against him has washed away with time.

Interestingly, the authorities have closed the cases and have no new plans to reopen them but it hasn't stopped an army of online sleuths and researchers attempting to solve them. So, who was responsible for the Templeton Woods murders?

World's End murders

In October 1977, 18 months before Carol Lannen's death, two 17-year-old girls were murdered on different nights in Edinburgh, 60 miles from Dundee. They were both last seen leaving the World's End Pub in the city's old town. Their killer was Angus Sinclair.

He had previously killed his eight-year-old neighbour in 1961, for which he served 10 years inside. In 1982, he pleaded guilty to the rape and assault of 11 children aged six to 14 and was sentenced to life in prison.

In 2001, he was first charged with the World's End murders, but after various controversies with botched forensics, he was acquitted. An amendment to the double jeopardy law later saw him convicted of the murders in 2014, along with the 1978 murder of 17-year-old Mary Gallacher in Glasgow.

Then, he was linked to four other young women killed in Scotland between 1977 and 1978, leading to some suspecting he was the Templeton Woods murderer. But police records show that Sinclair was in custody for a firearms charge at the time of both women's deaths. However, many prisoners were allowed out on work release, with much of the work release program going unrecorded in the late 1970s.

Partner in crime

Sinclair was so certain about the similarities between the murders that he feared being charged with both Templeton Woods deaths, due to the circumstantial evidence. Carol's purse and clothing were found on the riverbank near Aberdeen, a city where Sinclair was working in a motel before his firearm arrest – and after.

The photofit was a close match to his appearance, and the fact he had been convicted of four murders and multiple rapes, led some to believe he was the killer. But if Sinclair was in custody at the time, and had not been given work release – which is unrecorded – then who killed them?

Sinclair was known to have a partner in crime, named Gordon Hamilton, who helped him lure his victims, and also killed on his own. Could it be that the Templeton Woods deaths were copycat killings, designed to look like the World's End murders, to cover Sinclair's tracks?

Whatever further secrets Sinclair had, died with him in 2019, while serving his sentence.

Zodiac Killer

For many, the Zodiac Killer is one of the most infamous cold cases in America, if not the world. Between December 1968 and October 1969, in San Francisco, five people were killed by an unidentified serial killer.

The killer gave himself the moniker of Zodiac by sending taunting letters to local newspapers, many of which contained strange ciphers and codes. In one of the letters, the killer claimed to have murdered 37 victims.

After the last known murder, the Zodiac Killer disappeared and theories about what happened to him have perpetuated online. Other murders across the world have been connected to the Zodiac Killer, including sprees in Italy, Germany, and for some – Scotland.

In 2009, Tayside Major Crimes Investigations received a dossier that had been researched by an unidentified author, claiming that the Zodiac Killer had left California for Scotland in the mid-1970s, and that he was still living in the country.

Zodiac's last act

The conveniently unknown author claimed to have identified an American man living in the north-east of Scotland as the prime suspect in the Zodiac killings. According to the author's research, the man was responsible for Carol's death, and suspected in Elizabeth's.

In 2015, the author sent an email to a Scottish newspaper, and with regards to Carol's murder, claimed, '*this criminal act is often referred to as the first of 'The Templeton Woods Murders' my research formed a case study, which I submitted to Tayside CID in October 2009.*'

'*As a result, an investigation was carried out into the suspect. Although stood down after six months, the suspect remains, to this day, 'under review'. There was no sex on the agenda, and it appears that empowerment was the motive. This I believe, was Zodiac's last act and had a different motive to the crimes in California.*'

Though the Templeton Woods murder cases are seen as closed, authorities continue to log any new information that comes in. The killings could have been carried out by the Zodiac Killer, Angus Sinclair's partner, or an unidentified local man.

Perhaps the murders of Carol and Elizabeth were unconnected and it was merely a coincidence they were found so close together. Their deaths remain unsolved, and their killer or killers unidentified. Though it doesn't stop bizarre theories continuing to be talked about.

Templeton Woods continues to haunt investigators and true crime fans, as it has done for the past 40 years. It is one of Scotland's most infamous cold cases, and as time ticks on, the window for solving it gets ever smaller.

The Other Bathory

One of history's worst female murderers had a hobby of torturing and killing slaves, but escaped justice due to her wealth and connections, before becoming revered in Chilean culture.

It's easy to forget how diverse the historical true crime landscape is, and those from non-English backgrounds, of which Elizabeth Bathory is the most well-known, never really get the attention that perhaps their cases deserve.

Enter Catalina de los Ríos y Lísperguer, who was said to have been nicknamed La Quintrala due to her bright and flaming red hair. Some researchers write that La Quintrala comes from the Quintral plant, as she used the branches of the plant to whip her victims, and that its flowers were red, like her hair.

Catalina was a landowner and member of the aristocracy in 17th Century Chile. But don't let that upper class innocence fool you. Catalina's life was one of murder, cruelty, and lust.

Her hobby was torturing and killing many of the hundreds of slaves she had under her command. She also tried to kill her father, ordered a priest's assassination, and stabbed another priest in order to redeem her soul.

Born in 1604 to Spanish general Don Gonzalo de los Ríos and his wife María Lisperguer y Flores, Catalina was raised at the tail-end of the Conquest of Chile. María worked as a financer to Spanish Conquistador Pedro Gutiérrez de Valdiva, who became the first royal governor of Chile

Don Gonzalo was already part of the aristocracy and had accumulated a lot of land in Chile's capital, Santiago, where he became one of the colonial society's richest members. He owned various sugar cane farms that utilised black slaves to work them.

For Catalina, growing up in such an environment, where she was protected from the harshness of Chile's slums, and witness to the inhumanity of keeping slaves, it was no surprise she carved out the cruel life she would eventually lead. She had one sister and six brothers, none of whom turned out like her.

Despite being raised in a rich and fortunate family, Catalina didn't get a good education and was known to be illiterate until her death. Her mother was out of the picture when she was young, and she was mostly raised by her father and grandparents.

Catalina grew up to be held in high esteem across Santiago due to her heritage and unusual looks. She was tall, had sheer white skin, green eyes, and memorable flaming red hair. Her heritage was said to have been a mix of German, Spanish, and Incan, though her ancestry is confused when looking at ancestral records. Still, she cut a fine figure in 17th Century Chile.

Her path to cruelty was sped up by known practitioners of witchcraft within her family. Her grandmother, Águeda Flores, and one of her unnamed aunts, taught Catalina elements of witchcraft when she was a child and imbibed it further into her teenage years.

This combination of privilege and alternative teachings led to Catalina attempting to kill her father when she was just 18-years-old. In 1622, she prepared a dish of chicken for her father and laced it with poison.

Don Gonzalo was bedridden for weeks afterwards but went onto survive. One of Catalina's family members reported the poisoning to law officials but due to a lack of evidence – or her family's influence in the new colonial society – no charges were brought against her.

Aged 22, Catalina married a Spanish Colonel named Alonso Campofrío de Carvajal y Riberos, 20 years her senior. Alonso was paid handsomely by Catalina's grandmother, for taking Catalina off her hands, and in the hope the marriage may have calmed down her violent ways. It was not to be.

Frustrated that the marriage felt forced upon her, Catalina went to the home of the priest who married them and stabbed him in the stomach under cover of night. The priest went on to survive but it was only a taster of what Catalina was building up to.

She had a son with Alonso, who died of natural causes when he was eight-years-old. While Alonso moved from the military to the government and began to rise the ranks there, Catalina was taking lovers in secret.

In 1624, she invited a rich feudal lord to her dwellings. As they fornicated in one of her bedrooms, she slipped out some knives from behind the pillow and stabbed him multiple times. Some of the knives were said to have remained embedded in him when the body was found.

Catalina blamed the murder on one of her black slaves, who was eventually executed in public for the crime. In 1628, Catalina's only sister died, and she assumed control of her sister's vast estates and land. As more and more land fell under her control, tales of her cruelty were beginning to spread.

She stabbed another potential lover for refusing her sexual advances, then bragged about his sexual inadequacies to others. It was also claimed she cut off the ear of a sexual acquaintance named Martín de Ensenada, and murdered a Santiago Knight in front of another man, after a failed date.

After her father died, Catalina became one of the wealthiest landowners in all of Chile and made her home in one of the vast estates at the base of the Santiago mountains. She even owned land beyond the Andes range to the East of the country.

Like Bathory, her vast amount of land and wealth was a gateway to act out the very darkest of desires. Catalina took full control of the slaves that worked the land she now owned, and in doing so, personally managed the activities of all her estates and properties.

With no apparent motive, she killed a black slave named Ñatucón-Jetón and left his body to rot in the open air for a fortnight before ordering the remains to be buried. It was said that his body was left on the open fields to put the fear of God into other slaves that lived and worked nearby.

In 1633, a visiting priest, who had heard of Catalina's viciousness, approached her to change her ways, but she stabbed him and beat him to within an inch of his life. When word got around of the priest's beating, many slaves and tenants of her properties eloped into the mountains – which displeased Catalina.

She ordered a militia contingent to head into the Andes and bring back the slaves by force. They were all brought back to her estate at the base of the mountains. Though stories of what happened next have been embellished to some degree, it is known that each of the elopers were punished.

Many were tortured with knives and whipped with the branches of the Quintral parasitic plant. It remains unknown how many were killed during the torture. Catalina paid off local lawyers and judges and protected herself within the veil of her aristocratic family, to avoid prosecution for torture and murder, and it worked – for a while.

In 1634, a secret investigatory team was put together at the behest of the Royal Audience; the two Spanish colonial courts that represented administrative and political authority.

The lead investigator was Justice Francisco de Millán, who managed to talk to many of the slaves and tenants in secret. Almost all of them accused Catalina of torture, murder, and extreme violence. Some also pointed Francisco to the locations where bodies were buried.

Convinced he had enough evidence, Francisco had Catalina arrested and taken to Santiago for a criminal trial that was to throw the aristocracy into disrepute. She was charged with 40 murders, but it was claimed dozens more had died by her hand.

Due to her influence and wealth, the trial moved slowly, and after being paid off, the judges stalled the case and Catalina was released. At the same time, her husband, though aware of her actions, decided to ignore the stories, and proclaimed his love for her right up until his death in 1650.

She brushed his death off like nothing, as if wiping the blood of her slaves from her shoulder. In 1662, a new trial began, as many officials were scrambling to discover the extent of Catalina's crimes, believing the murders to number vastly more than the 40 originally laid at her feet.

Unknown to officials at the time, Catalina had been getting away with torturing slaves and murdering some of them for almost 30 years, since the first trial was abandoned.

Catalina became ill, and in 1665, aged 61, died from natural causes, taking many of her dark secrets to the grave. But then something strange happened. In her will, she left 20,000 pesos to the Church of San Agustin for 20,000 masses to be held for her own death and the lives of her slaves and tenants.

She instructed that her assets were auctioned for the benefit of the people of Santiago and the Augustinians. Her funeral was a lavish affair, attracting aristocracy and commoners alike. She was buried in the Church of San Agustín, but the exact location of her tomb remains a secret.

When her exploits and cruelty became public knowledge, many of her estates and properties were abandoned, as people believed her evil spirit resided in them. She lives on in Chilean culture today as both a revered and iconic image.

Despite her violence, she ended up becoming one of Chile's most infamous historical female figures, due to her power within a male-dominated Chile. She was alive at a time when women generally held supporting roles for the men around them.

Her farms, plantations, and estates were crucial to the economy of colonial Chile, and it remains the only possible reason why she was never legally brought to justice, despite the evidence of mass torture, brutality, and murder.

Unlike Bathory, La Quintrala left much of her wealth to the church, Order of St. Augustine, and the people of Santiago, but it still doesn't wipe out the ghoulish nature of her crimes against other humans. She remains one of history's most brutal female murderers, horrific and yet – immortal.

The Beenham Child Killer

A child killer claimed two young lives, shocking a small Berkshire village, but the killer was a local who had already claimed another victim six months earlier, and would escape justice for 45 years.

1960s Britain was infamous for a number of child killers, not least the Moors Murderers and the Cannock Chase Monster, but there was another who was convicted of two murders and were it not for the hard work of cold case investigators, would have got away with a third.

The small village of Beenham in Berkshire traces its roots to the 12th Century when it became a Church of England Parish, with Saint Mary's church being the focal point of the community. Jump forward 900 years and the population of the village remains below 500.

Over a six month period from 1966 to 1967, three murders took place that shocked not only the community but the entire nation. It focussed attention on Beenham in such a way that the village has never really escaped the shadow of what became known as the Beenham Murders.

The killer, David Burgess, was caught just weeks after the last murder and was convicted in 1967 for the murder of two nine-year-old girls – two of the three Beenham victims. The other victim, six months earlier, was a 17-year-old who was not connected to Burgess at the time.

It was 45 years later in 2011 when the 17-year-old victim was connected to him. When interviewed by police accusing him of the murder, he calmly looked up from the interview table, smiled, and said '*prove it*.'

At the tail-end of a cold October in 1966, 17-year-old Kent-born Yolande Waddington took a job as a nanny with the Jagger family in Beenham. The location was accessible as Yolande lived with her parents only nine miles away in nearby Newbury.

Yolande's vocation in life was to become a children's nurse and nannying was one of the routes to take in the 1960s, experience over education tended to bring social jobs within easier reach. The Jagger family ran Oakwood Farm and needed assistance with their children, and Yolande was the perfect choice.

Becoming a live-in nanny at a young age, though Yolande's dream, tended to cut them off from their own social circles. So it was met with delight from the Jagger family that Yolande's own family was only a few miles away.

On 28th October 1966, after only three days of working with the Jagger's, Yolande would meet an untimely demise. She spent the evening writing a letter to her boyfriend then shortly after 10pm, when the children were asleep, she walked away from the farm and down the road to the post box, 15 minutes away.

At 10.35pm, she jumped into the Six Bells pub, a local drinking haven, and bought some cigarettes. It was the last time anyone saw her alive – apart from her killer. The following morning, when the Jagger parents found their live-in nanny had not returned from the night before, they became concerned.

They phoned Yolande's boyfriend who said he hadn't heard from her and had no idea where she was. Shortly before noon on the 29th, the Jagger's phoned the police and a search got underway. Less than 24 hours after that, and a day before

Halloween, Beenham was about to be scarred by its first of three brutal murders.

After an intensive search of the village and surrounding fields, and in the late morning of the 30th, two farm workers traipsed into a cow shed on the outskirts of the village and made a macabre discovery. Beside some bales of hay, they found bloodstained items of clothing.

Realising the clothes may have belonged to the missing girl, they searched around the shed and just a short distance away in a nearby ditch, they found the brutalised body of Yolande. A large scale murder investigation was launched that at the time was the largest Berkshire had ever seen.

Yolande was found half-nude and had been tied at the wrists by baling twine, a hemp-like thin rope that's used to tie hay bales together. An autopsy showed that she had been strangled to death with the same cord, stabbed twice in the chest, and left for dead within an hour of leaving the pub.

Unusually, the stab wounds were only two inches deep and it appeared the killer had stabbed her with a small penknife merely to subdue her before killing by strangulation. It was unusual as most murders by knife are carried out with much larger blades.

Detectives were shipped in from across the county along with some officers from Scotland Yard. A search of the area was carried out by them and United States Airmen who were based at USAF Greenham Common – now RAF Greenham – just ten miles away from Beenham.

Within a day of the murder, a broken blade belonging to a pen knife was found a few hundred metres from the cow shed and it had remnants of blood on it. Testing of the blood on the blade and on her clothing uncovered two different blood groups, one belonging to Yolande, the other to the killer.

The local police stepped up their investigation and interviewed approximately 4,000 people, including everyone from the village and many from the surrounding areas. In the days before DNA testing, blood testing and fingerprints were one of the primary forensic methods.

To that effect, the police set up the first mass blood testing drive in UK investigation history. They set up a testing centre and requested that every adult male from the age of 16 in and around the village of Beenham had to give a sample of their blood.

By early November 1966, just two weeks after the murder, over 200 blood samples had been submitted and tested by forensic scientists. Four men were found to have the same blood type as the blood at the scene but due to various alibis and other evidence, were discounted as suspects.

One suspect, who would one day come back to haunt the investigation, was 19-year-old David Burgess. He had been in the pub when Yolande had come in for cigarettes and was known to have had around 14 pints of beer.

He claimed that he left the pub shortly after Yolande but saw her walk away and nothing else. His blood type didn't exactly match, with only three of the four testing aspects coming up as positive. For that reason, Burgess was removed from the suspect list, and it would be 45 years before the truth came out.

By early 1967, the investigation had started to run on empty. With no new evidence or suspects to look at, the case went cold but it never closed. Then, as the horrors of Yolande's mysterious murder began to pass into the realm of the unsolved, a new horror was awaiting Beenham.

On 17th April 1967, shortly after the bell rang signalling the end of the school day, two nine-year-old school friends, Jeanette Wigmore and Jacqueline Williams, jumped on their bicycles and began the short ride home.

They went to Jeanette's home, where her father, Tony, saw the two girls playing near the lane at the back of the house. It was the last time they were ever seen alive.

By 6:45pm when dinner was waiting on the table and Jeanette hadn't come in from the cool Spring evening, her father went to Jacqueline's family home to look for her. When both families realised the girls were missing, they informed other locals who put together a search party.

Remembering that Jeanette liked to play at a local gravel pit called Blake's Pit opposite a quarry site called Fisher's gravel pits, Tony drove there ahead of other searchers and parked up. At 8.30pm, he found both bicycles lying flat on the ground. A short distance away, he discovered the body of his daughter, face down in water at the bottom of a bank.

When the local search party descended on Blake's Pit, they found Jacqueline's body just 100 metres away from Jeanette's, also face down in water and hurriedly covered with leaves and twigs. The time of death of both girls was in the hour before dinner was served at the Wigmore household.

Once again, Beenham was home to cold-blooded murder. Autopsies showed that Jeanette had been stabbed five times in the chest and throat, while

Jacqueline was sexually assaulted and strangled by the killer's bare hands before being drowned in a small pool of water.

For the second time in six months, Scotland Yard sent a team of officers and another 80 or so specially trained police to Beenham. The entirety of the gravel pit and the waters were drained by specialist teams looking for the murder weapon which was never found.

The investigation involved the entire village and surrounding areas where almost 1,500 statements were taken and hundreds more interviews carried out. Fear had taken hold of Beenham and many residents took their children out of school until the killer was caught.

It seemed to be no coincidence that the murder of Yolande and the two school friends were so close together, and many villagers were confident it was the same culprit behind them. The police continued their investigation of the gravel pit and attempted to create a timeline of the entire village from the statements that had been provided.

They discovered that two local brothers were working at the quarry at the time and brought them in for questioning. John Burgess said that he and the last of his colleagues had left Fishers gravel pits at around 6pm but his brother, dumper driver

David Burgess, had gone to Blake's Pit to check some of his rabbit-snares as he was a rabbit hunter in his spare time.

Beenham-born Burgess had returned 20 minutes later and waited with some of the other workers before making their own way home. He was asked to hand over the clothing he was wearing that day to police but told them it already looked bad as he was near the area anyway.

Realising that Burgess had already been a suspect in Yolande's murder six months earlier, they doubled-down on him as the killer but needed proof. Fortunately for the two girl's families, evidence was easy to come by.

Jeannette's blood type was AB/MN, one of the rarest kinds. It was matched to unwashed blood splatter on a boot which Burgess had been wearing at work the day of the murder. With a blood match and the statement from his brother, Burgess was arrested and charged with the two girl's murders on 7th May 1967.

In less than 20 minutes, he had taken the lives of two girls playing happily in the shadow of their hometown. Just three days before his arrest and two weeks after the murders, Burgess was seen buying drinks for Jacqueline's father – knowing he had killed his daughter.

At his trial, Burgess came up with a story of witnessing an unidentified man standing over the body of one of the girls. The man, who he referred to as McNab, threatened him and his family with severe consequences should he say anything about what he had seen.

Unsurprisingly, the jury didn't believe him and found him guilty of both murders. He was given two life sentences and condemned to rot in jail for 29 years. As much as the police wanted to pin Yolande's murder on him, they simply didn't have the evidence needed and so her case went cold.

In May 1996, after 29 years in prison, Burgess was released on license but couldn't keep out of trouble. He failed to report back to prison and got involved in drunken behaviour. Then, in early 1998, he carried out an armed robbery on a bank in Havant, Hampshire, before being arrested in nearby Portsmouth. He was convicted and sentenced to another 10 years.

While in prison for the second time, he confessed to Yolande's murder but told the prison officers and subsequent investigating officers to *'prove it'*. While serving his time for armed robbery, he was given additional sentences for wounding another prisoner with intent back in 1978 and making false statements to receive benefits in 1996.

It seemed the police were wanting a way to keep him where they could watch him as they attempted to prove he had killed Yolande, and in 2010, the case was reopened. Using new DNA testing techniques, investigators discovered DNA on Yolande's clothes that matched Burgess's.

In early 2012, the then 64-year-old Burgess was convicted of her murder and sentenced to an additional 27 years in prison. 45 years after her death, Yolande and her family finally got the justice they deserved.

Police learned that he had followed Yolande from the Six Bell's pub before deciding to sexually assault her and killed her so she could never speak out against him. Jeanette and Jacqueline playing in the gravel pit were opportunistic murders that were carried out with no emotion or humanity.

For Beenham, their 1,000-year history would be forever tainted by the horrors of one of their own, a child killer who was no more than a child himself, hiding in plain sight.

Fortunately, Yolande's voice was finally heard, 45 years after her death, with the help of modern forensic technology, proving that justice will always find a way, and that criminals of any age will always be looking over their shoulder, waiting for the past to catch up.

The Black Panther

With over 400 thefts, 19 post office robberies, four murders, and countless assaults to his name, the Black Panther was Britain's most prolific criminal, known for the disturbing death of a kidnapped girl.

By the 1970s, post office robberies in Britain were on the increase, as criminals turned their attention away from banks to focus on mostly rural locations with minimal to zero security. Post office's general level of security was simply a sales counter between the customer and staff.

Donald Nielson was one of the more known post office robbers who hit dozens of establishments from 1971 to 1974. His case stands out above many others, as he murdered four people, including a young girl he kidnapped for ransom.

Nielson was born Donald Nappey in Bradford in August 1936 and quickly turned to crime. In 1947, when he was 10, Nielson's mother died of cancer and he was left alone with a father who didn't want him. At the same time, he was being bullied in school over his surname, which he hated.

He entered the criminal lifestyle a year later, aged 11, when he broke into a shop to rob the cash register, but was caught red-handed by police, who let him off with a caution due to his age, unaware of what the future was to hold.

When he was 17, he was conscripted into the army as part of the British National Service law that required healthy males to serve in the armed forces for 18 months and remain on the reserve list for four years.

A year later in 1955, he married the love of his life, Irene Tate, a woman two years older than he was. She convinced him to leave the army as soon as his 18-month service had come to an end. But Nielson relished the army lifestyle which had encouraged his love of guns and other weapons.

He left the army for his wife and set up a business making sheds at their home in Bradford. In 1960, they give birth to a daughter named Kathryn, and Nielson changed his surname to rid himself of his embarrassing family name and prevent similar bullying to his daughter.

The new surname was chosen because he had recently purchased a taxi business from a man named Nielson and liked the sound of it. It was a coincidence that he would be later confused with Dennis Nielsen, another serial killer who was active from 1978.

When Nielson was 29, in 1965, he was drawn back to his life of crime and became addicted to carrying out burglaries. It was estimated he had committed over 400 burglaries from 1965 to when he was finally caught in 1975.

He was aggrieved each time, as the proceeds from the crimes were small but knew that if he escalated too quickly that the police would be on to him. In the early days, he adapted his method of burglary to what the news was saying about him.

When he worked out that police had established a pattern of behaviour, he would change it up. On many occasions, he stole a radio and left it on the pavement near the property. When he read about the radio connection in the newspapers, he included a different calling card, such as leaving a tap on, or moving items in the house around.

In November 1970, realising the minimal returns were getting him nowhere, he broke into a large family home in Dewsbury, West Yorkshire, and stole two shotguns from the well-off family, including a large amount of ammunition.

During the year that followed, his burglaries became more violent as he fought homeowners and restrained others so he could get what he wanted. On every occasion, he wore a black mask and black clothing, and sometimes put on an accent in an attempt to outwit police. Before he was known as The Black Panther, the press referred to him as The Phantom, or Handy Andy.

In early 1971, he used one of the shotguns to rob a sub-post office in Barnsley and escaped with a little over £3,000, worth £50,000 today. Seeing the success of the raid, he robbed another post office in Rotherham where he made off with almost £4,000.

A few months later, he burgled a house in Cheshire and stole two automatic pistols, three rifles, and bags full of ammunition. He chose certain houses as he discovered they were either farmers or hunters, and as such were likely to have firearms on the premises.

Shortly after raiding the house, he held up a sub-post office in Mansfield, and made off with nearly £3,000. Nielson was beginning to amass a large amount of cash but couldn't escape the thrill of the crime.

In February 1972, he broke into a small post office in Heywood, Lancashire, which was attached to a small family home. The house and post office owner, Leslie Richardson, awoke in the middle of the night to find Nielson standing beside his bed with a shotgun.

Richardson, who had also served in the army, leapt out of bed to fight with the intruder. Nielson fought back and broke bones in Richardson's feet by stamping on them, before shooting him in the leg and eloping empty-handed. Richardson and his wife survived the attack.

From 1971 to 1974, he held up 19 post offices at gunpoint, and made off with thousands of pounds each time. By this point, the press had begun referring to him as The Black Panther, because a witness remarked on his speed, which was as fast as a panther, and the fact he was wearing all black clothing and a black mask.

The first murder to be linked to Nielson happened in February 1974, when he robbed a sub-post office in Harrogate. Owner Donald Skepper confronted Nielson, who lifted his shotgun and blasted him in the chest, killing him instantly.

Seven weeks later, he raided a post office in Baxenden, Lancashire and shot dead postmaster Derek Astin. Two months after Astin's death, and with the police hot on his trail, Nielson continued to carry out robberies and burglaries across Yorkshire, resulting in another murder.

In November 1974, Nielson robbed a post office in Langley, West Midlands, that belonged to Sidney Grayland and his wife Margaret, who lived on the premises. When Sidney attempted to fight Nielson off, he was shot dead. Nielson then beat Margaret with the butt of the shotgun to within an inch of her life. Fortunately, she survived the attack but was left with life-changing injuries.

Not content with having robbed tens of thousands of pounds and killing three people, Nielson came up with a plan that would go on to shock, not just Yorkshire, but the whole of the country.

A few years earlier, Nielson had read a news story about a 17-year-old girl named Lesley Whittle, who had been left £82,000 by her father, George, in his will to avoid estate taxes, worth £1.3million today. George had been a coach business owner and had amassed a large fortune off the back of it.

On 14th January 1975, after having planned it for many years, Nielson broke into Whittle's large home in Shropshire by cutting a telephone line connected to the house, which he suspected was a burglar alarm, then crept into the property through the garage

Though he had originally intended to kidnap Lesley's mother, Dorothy, as she too had been left a fortune, he instead decided to kidnap Lesley when he came across her room first. He gagged her as Dorothy was asleep in the next room, having taken sleeping pills the evening before.

Nielson kidnapped Lesley, who was the same age as his daughter, and tied her up on the back seat of car, before holding her captive, hoping to pick up a hefty ransom. He had left a ransom note on Lesley's bed demanded £50,000 for her return with detailed instructions of where to leave the cash and not to involve the police, thinking it would have been easy for the Whittle family to follow.

He drove Lesley to Bathpool Park in Kidsgrove, Staffordshire, 45 miles away. He led her to a deep drainage shaft connected to a nearby reservoir, before climbing down with her to a small platform, 16 metres below the surface.

He put a hood over her head, stripped her naked and secured her to the platform with wire around her neck. He provided her with a small mattress and sleeping bag and left her in the freezing darkness before going home to his wife and daughter.

Dorothy found the ransom note the next morning and phoned her step-son and Lesley's brother, Ronald Whittle. When he didn't pick up, she jumped in her car and sped over to the home that he shared with his wife, Gaynor, before bringing them back to the Whittle house.

Despite the ransom note stating not to contact the police, Ronald made the decision to call them. The note stated that one of the Whittle family members was to wait for a phone call at a public telephone box beside a shopping centre in Kidderminster that evening.

The police and press became involved in a big way and were ultimately responsible for a serious of errors that messed up the ransom delivery. Some journalists realised the local police were involved in something big, uncovered the story and released it to news channels the same evening.

As midnight came, and Nielson hadn't called the phone box, both the police and press feared the worst. Then at 1am on January 16th, Nielson phoned and played a tape message with Lesley's voice, claiming she was okay but stated that a Whittle family member should go to a second phone box where there were instructions hidden behind it.

24 hours later, in the early hours of the 17th, Ronald Whittle drove to the second phone box with £50,000 in a suitcase but got lost and went 1.5 miles off course due to police not giving him the correct directions.

Half hour later, he reached the destination and found the note that instructed him to walk to the next lane in Bathpool Park, flash the car lights, then look out for torch light at the end of the lane.

He followed the instructions, but there was no sign of Nielson, even after Ronald exited the vehicle and shouted. Nielson had been spooked by a routine patrol car that had passed near the lane just minutes before Ronald arrived.

The blame was placed squarely on the police for not changing the route of the car, as the officer driving had no idea about the drop. Police searched the park the next day but didn't find any evidence, missing the drain shaft where Lesley was being kept. As a result of the mess up, they ordered a media blackout.

The same night of the failed ransom drop, a security guard called Gerald Smith had been shot six times in the back and was recovering in hospital. A car was located near the scene that had a tape recorder with Lesley's voice on it, and other evidence linking to Nielson but West Midlands police didn't find out until one week later.

As the hunt for the kidnapper went into a second week, forensic experts confirmed that the evidence found in the car, and the bullets that were pulled out of Gerald, matched those used in The Black Panther robberies and murders.

On 6th March, a school headmaster informed police that a pupil had handed him a note that mentioned dropping a suitcase into a hole, along with a flashlight wedged into the grill of a drainage shaft. Police then descended on Bathpool Park, a location they had already searched.

When gas experts confirmed the shafts were safe to open, police entered them. 14 metres down in the third shaft, they found a tape recorder on a flat surface which suggested Nielson had used the shaft to hide Lesley.

On the third landing, 16 metres down, they found the mattress and sleeping bag, but below the landing, Lesley's nude and decomposing body was hanging from the steel wire by her neck, with her toes only six inches from the bottom of the shaft. When the body was found, the lead investigator, Chief Superintendent Bob Booth, was demoted to a street officer for the succession of failures.

There were two theories relating to Lesley's death, one that Nielson had re-entered the shaft to push her to her death, and another that he never returned and she either took her own life or died in an accident when she fell.

An autopsy suggested she had died from vagal inhibition, which occurs when pressure is placed on the vagus nerve in the neck, causing the brain to slow down the heart. In Lesley's case, her heart stopped altogether, leading to her death.

They also discovered she had not consumed any food or water for three days prior to her death, due to her stomach and intestines being empty, and may have been alive for up to seven days before she died.

In December 1975, 11 months after Lesley's death which had shocked the nation, two officers on road duty were sitting in their car in Mansfield, when they spotted a suspicious looking man carrying a holdall. They approached him to search the bag but he pulled out a shotgun and ordered them back into the car.

They had unknowingly been accosted by Nielson, who ordered them to drive to another town six miles away. When they approached a junction beside a fish and chip takeaway, the officer behind the wheel slammed on the brakes but the gun went off, hitting him in the hand.

The car came to a screeching halt and the other officer called for help. Two men who were queuing at the takeaway ran to the police car to assist and eventually they all overpowered Nielson. They dragged him to iron railings on the side of the road and handcuffed him as back-up arrived.

After all the evidence had emerged, Nielson was charged with four murders, multiple robberies, theft of weapons, kidnapping, and assault. In Lesley's case, Nielson pleaded not guilty to murder, but instead pleaded guilty to manslaughter.

At his trial in July 1976, Nielson was found guilty of Lesley's murder and told by the judge that the *'enormity of his crimes put him in a class apart from almost all other convicted murderers in recent years.'*

He was sentenced to life for the murder of Lesley, and another four life sentences for the three other murders and attack on Margaret Grayland. He received an additional 21 years for the kidnapping, 10 years for blackmail, and another 30 years for theft and weapons offences.

It was clear that Nielson would never leave prison alive and would meet the end of his days inside. Gerald the security guard died of his wounds one year later but a conviction was not pursued as it wouldn't have changed the ultimate outcome of a whole life tariff.

In 2008, aged 72, Nielson appealed to lower his sentence but it was refused by the Home Secretary, and the whole life tariff was upheld. In 2011, Nielson died in hospital of natural causes, and for the hundreds of families affected by his crimes, they were finally able to breathe a sigh of relief.

Body in the Garden

A ten-year-old girl was abducted and murdered in Notting Hill, leading to a 100-year-old cold case, which despite a strong suspect and solid investigatory work, remains officially unsolved to this day.

Vera was a 10-year-old girl who lived in Notting Hill with her family. On the day of her murder, 14th December 1931, she was visiting nearby relatives when she left to walk the 50-metre distance home. It was the last time she was seen alive.

After a large search of the area, a milkman discovered her body in the undergrowth of a garden two days later, a mile away from her home. She had been raped and manually strangled to death. Despite a large and ongoing investigation into her murder, no suspect has ever been caught and her murder remains unsolved.

Born to a working class family in Hammersmith, London, on 13th April 1921, she was raised as an only child by parents who doted on her. Her father, Charles Page, was a railway worker, and her mother, Isabel, stayed at home as a housewife, a product of 1920s England, they moved to a small property in Notting Hill shortly after Vera's birth.

To supplement the family income, Isabel would take in lodgers but they were usually people known to the family, rather than all-out strangers. In January 1931, they moved to a larger three-storey house in Notting Hill, where they resided in rooms across the lower two floors, with other residents above them.

Arthur and Annie Rush were one of the couple's that lived above them and had been there for over two decades when the Page's moved in. One of their sons, 41-year-old Percival Orlando Rush, would frequent the property on many occasions and would eventually become the prime suspect in Vera's disappearance.

Murder & the milkman

On that fateful afternoon in 1931, aged 10, Vera disappeared on the walk back home after visiting her auntie. When she failed to return home, the alarm was raised. It had only been 45 minutes from the time she had left her aunties home to the time she was known to be missing.

Less than an hour was all it took for her abductor to remove her from her family and the life she knew. By 10.30pm, Charles reported his daughter missing to police. He helped put together a search team of relatives and locals to look for her and they worked through the night to no avail.

By the following morning on the 15th, the press had got wind of the story and soon enough the disappearance of Vera Page had gone national. Despite being seen by a school-friend near a chemist, no-one else had seen her in the short distance from her auntie's house to her family home.

In the dark early hours of the morning on the 16th, Joseph Smith, a milkman returning from his duties, stumbled across something he never expected to see. In the front garden of a home near to Holland Park, he saw the body of a child in the undergrowth, covered by her own coat.

There had been no attempt to hide the body and it was on full display for everyone to see. Realising what he was looking at and stunned by the marble-like complexion of the child's face, Joseph raised the alarm.

When police identified the body as Vera's, the abduction became a murder investigation. Distraught at their loss, Vera's parents did all they could to help find the killer, by speaking about it in the press and helping investigators at every turn.

Unfortunately, it meant that Charles became a suspect in his daughter's death but police needed proof. Wedged against Vera's inner elbow were the remnants of a finger bandage with traces of ammonia, which would later prove vital in seeking a suspect. It appeared the killer had a bandage on his finger that had come off when he placed the body in the garden.

A local killer

An autopsy was carried out which unearthed new details. Due to the variation in weather in the two days from being abducted to being found, it was concluded that Vera's body had been kept with her captor for the two days she was missing.

Using the weather patterns and corresponding it with the amount of weathering on Vera's body, it suggested she had been dumped in the undergrowth just two hours before she was discovered.

The autopsy found traces of coal dust and candle wax on her coat and body, which led investigators to believe she had been kept in a coal shed or cellar until being removed and placed in the garden. This combined with the bandage added to an ever-growing stack of evidence, except they had no suspect.

It was confirmed that Vera had been raped and manually strangled to death in the hours following her disappearance, which meant she had lain dead for at least 40 hours.

Detectives believed the man was local to the area, as he would not have been able to keep Vera's body for two days and place her in the garden if he didn't know the area. The placement of the body, away from prying eyes but in a very public location meant that the killer had good local geographical knowledge.

The owner of the house and the milkman confirmed the timeline of when the body must have been placed. The owner, who was an early-riser, collected the milk from the milkman at 5.30am. Neither the milkman nor the owner saw the body then.

When the milkman was returning along the same road at 7.50am, he noticed the body. The owner said she would have seen it before 5.30am if it had been there. This meant the killer had a two hour window to secretly place the body in the garden.

Large investigation

Due to the public outrage at the murder, the pressure on police to find the killer was mounting but the outpouring of grief led to thousands of people attending Vera's funeral. The investigation went house to house around Notting Hill, Kensington, and Holland Park, to speak to as many people as they could.

Over the coming weeks, police took approximately 3,000 witness statements and interviewed over 1,000 people in relation to the murder. Nothing solid came up until one of the later witness statements gave hope that the killer was about to be caught.

At 6.30am on the morning of the 16th, a homeowner was looking out her window when she saw a local man pushing a full wheelbarrow, with its contents covered by a red tablecloth. The homeowner didn't think anything of it until the police spoke to her.

The local man she saw was Percival *'Percy'* Orlando Rush – whose parents lived on the floor above the Page's home. Another witness said that the door to a large coal shed near to where the body was discovered was left open on the morning of the discovery.

The coal shed had no electrical lighting which meant only candles could be used to illuminate the shed, one of the ways that caused traces of candle wax to be found on Vera's body. With the name of a possible suspect, the location the body was stored in, and solid witness statements, police went all in on Percy Rush.

Percival Rush

Rush was a married 41-year-old launderette worker who came into contact with ammonia on a daily basis. He used to live in the same property as the Page's and would regularly return to visit his parents on the top floor, which meant he had a key to the property.

Rush admitted that he talked to Vera many times but had not seen her in the weeks leading up to her murder. More importantly for the investigation, Rush had damaged his little finger a few days before Vera was killed, and had worn a finger bandage, similar to the one that had been found wedged underneath Vera's elbow.

Two days after the body was found, Rush was arrested and questioned at Notting Hill police station where he proclaimed his innocence but agreed with what the police had found out. He didn't deny hurting his finger or knowing Vera but denied he was the killer.

With circumstantial evidence laid at his feet, Rush was charged with the murder and sent to trial but it didn't go to plan for the prosecution, as there simply was not enough evidence to convict him. Rush had hurt his finger at work on the 9th of December and his colleagues said he took it off a couple of days later and was not wearing one on the 14th, the day of Vera's disappearance.

The bandage found on Vera was a perfect fit for Rush's finger but according to a forensic analyst the material used was slightly different to the samples taken from Rush's home during a search by police.

Due to a procedural error, when going house to house, police had told Rush about the bandage, before he was a suspect, which would have given Rush ample time to get rid of any evidence. If Rush was the killer, then the release of confidential information by the police may have resulted in Rush getting away with it.

Unidentified murderer

Despite the witness seeing him pushing a wheelbarrow, there were no other witness statements putting him in the road where the garden was at the time the body was dumped. Local chemists reported they didn't sell Rush or his family the type of bandage found at the scene.

The owner of the coal shed was Thomas O'Conner who had ended his tenancy on it five days before the murder. He had taken the shed's padlocks with him which meant the coal shed would have been unlocked before the body was placed there.

There was simply not enough evidence to prove Rush had killed Vera. The jury agreed that the evidence was circumstantial at best, leading to Rush's acquittal.

For decades after, Rush was vilified as the killer of Vera, despite being acquitted of murder. He died in Ealing in 1961, having claimed his innocence at every opportunity. He had left the courts as a free man but no other suspect was found, and if Rush had killed her then he got away with murder.

If he didn't, then an unidentified killer was let free to walk the streets of Central London, and with the type of murder it was, it wouldn't have been a surprise if the killer had struck again, somewhere and at some time in history. Vera Page's abduction and murder remains officially unsolved.

The West's

A cruel tale of serial killing, abuse, and Britain's most evil couple, Fred and Rose West, who buried the bodies of their victims under the patio in their garden.

Fred West, in league with his wife, Rosemary West, would take the lives of at least 12 young women before being arrested in 1994. Their address of 25 Cromwell Street became synonymous with the murders and became known as the House of Horrors in the British press.

So much public hate was subsequently directed towards the House of Horrors, that Gloucester City Council intervened. They purchased the property for £40,000 in 1996, in the knowledge that no one would live there. They then unceremoniously destroyed the property, and with it, any physical trace of the horrors that had haunted the building.

During their uniquely evil relationship, Fred and Rose buried the remains of nine victims under their patio in the garden of 25 Cromwell Street, including their daughter, Heather. Fred's eight-year-old stepdaughter was unearthed at his previous home in Midland Road, Gloucester.

Fred's first wife and a childminder were found buried in shallow graves in remote locations outside the city limits. The 12 victims in total are the ones we know about, whose lives were ended in the most horrific of ways, with many being decapitated and dismembered. Police have long suspected that the bones of further victims are buried in and around Gloucester.

The formation of evil

Fred West was born in 1941 and raised during World War Two, the first child to a family of poor farm workers in Herefordshire. His father was strict and his mother overprotective, leading to him becoming known as a mummy's boy.

By 1951, the West's had six surviving children, as two had died within months of being born. Each of the children were given chores on the farm but Fred developed a habit of thieving. His mother sexually abused him and forced him to engage in sex acts with animals in his early teen years. His father also had open sexual relationships with Fred's younger sisters, which instilled a notion in Fred that incest was normal.

At the age of 17, a year after leaving school, he crashed his motorbike and remained unconscious for a week in hospital with a fractured skull and many broken bones. From then, he became prone to fits of extreme rage and anger.

In 1961, when he was 20, his 13-year-old sister, Kitty, told her parents that Fred had been raping her since she was 12. As word got around, Fred was arrested, but told police that he had been raping and sexually abusing young girls because it was a normal thing to do and everybody did it. The case was thrown out when Kitty refused to testify.

From then, Fred was abandoned by his family, and so he sought to create his own. He married his first wife, Catherine Bernadette Costello, in November 1962 at an empty wedding ceremony. Catherine gave birth to a mix-raced child, Charmaine, from her first relationship and Fred's first daughter, Anna Marie in 1964.

While living in Glasgow, the West's nanny, Isa McNeill, said the two girls were kept in cages on their bunk beds and only let out when Fred was at work. In 1965, Fred ran over and killed a young boy with his ice cream van but it was considered an accident and he was freed of any wrongdoing. A few months later, he took Charmaine and Anna Marie to his new home, a rented caravan in Gloucester.

Fred had met his first murder victim, Ann McFall, in Glasgow when she was 16, a friend of the nanny. By the time she was 18, she was living in Fred's caravan and was pregnant with his child. While she was pregnant, she disappeared and was never seen again – until June 1994, when her remains were unearthed in a cornfield. It was suggested her unborn child was cut from her womb as she was still alive.

Crossing of dark souls

In 1969, the then 29-year-old Fred, met 15-year-old Rosemary Letts at a bus stop, and over the coming months, after showering her with gifts, she moved into his caravan as an informal nanny to Anna Marie and Charmaine. Rose's family disapproved of the relationship, including her father, Bill Letts, who was diagnosed with schizophrenia. And yet, Rose's path to evil had also been marred by abuse.

When Rose's mother was pregnant with her, she underwent electroconvulsive therapy for her depression, which some say caused prenatal injuries to Rose. From the age of 14, Rose would walk around the house naked and was known to have abused her two younger brothers. It was also claimed but never proven that Rose was raped by her own father in her formative years, which caused her to abuse her siblings.

Fred was imprisoned in December 1970 for the theft of car tyres and remained in prison until June 1971. Rose gave birth to their first child together, Heather, a few months before. During Fred's sentence, while in their new flat at Midland Road, Gloucester, Charmaine and Anna Marie were subjected to physical and sexual abuse from Rose. A few days before Fred's release, Rose killed Charmaine and stored her body in the coal cellar.

When Fred was released, he cut off Charmaine's fingers and buried the body in the back yard of the block of flats. Later on, it would remain unclear for a while who exactly had killed Charmaine but evidence proved that Fred West was serving his sentence at the time of her death.

In August 1971, Catherine went to Gloucester to confront Fred about the custody of her children and was never seen alive again. Her body was uncovered many years later in a small wood. She had been dismembered and the body parts placed into different plastic bags. As with most of Fred's victims, her fingers had been removed, and likely kept by him as mementos of the crimes.

Murdering as a pair

By January 1972, when Rose was pregnant with their second child, the West's moved into 25 Cromwell Street, a rented council property that Fred later purchased from the council for around £7,000. As part of the purchase, he turned the upper floor rooms into bedsits to take lodgers to help pay for the ever-growing West family. Rose and Fred married at the end of the same month and gave birth to Mae June in the Summer.

Over the years, Rose turned to prostitution and used a room in the house to entertain her clients, complete with peepholes that allowed Fred – and his children – to watch. By 1983, Rose had given birth to eight children, some of them black, as they were the offspring of some of her clients. Many of the children were killed by her and Fred.

At least eight of the victims had been raped, tortured, and mutilated. Before being murdered, they were used in violent sexual fantasies where bondage played a heavy part in the household. They would then dismember the bodies and bury them in the cellar and garden of 25 Cromwell Street.

Before Cromwell Street, Fred had killed two on his own and Rosemary killed one; Charmaine. The rest of their victims were killed as a pair. The level of control they asserted over others is as horrific as it is shocking.

Rose would also engage in casual sex with both male and female lodgers. It was stated that when she had sex with other women, Rose would become more violent as the control slipped. She would partially suffocate them and insert exceptionally large sex objects inside them.

If they cried or showed fear or pain then Rose would become more excited. Shockingly, when Rose's father found out about her prostitution, he would regularly visit her to have sex with his own daughter. It was clear that both Fred and Rose took to extreme levels of sexual perversity, and it was this that resulted in the deaths of so many.

Fred West also collected VHS videos that showed bestiality and child abuse. It has always remained unclear how he was sourcing these types of tapes but they were surely a catalyst to even more crimes. Since the marriage in 1972, the sexual violence increased.

It became shocking to many that the crimes were going mostly unseen in what was a busy residential street.

Everybody does it

All of the West's children were abused in some form or another. They took 'great care' not to mark the children's faces or hands when they assaulted them. Any admittance to hospitals were explained away as accidents and never reported. All the children witnessed the abuse inflicted on each other and regular sexual abuse became the norm.

From the age of eight, Anna Marie, Fred's daughter via Catherine, was subjected to horrific abuse. She was dragged to the cellar of 25 Cromwell Street and had her clothes torn off. She was tied naked to a mattress and gagged before Fred raped her as Rose egged him on – this became a regular occurrence.

"Everybody does it to every girl. It's a father's job. Don't say anything to anybody." - Rose West, to Anna Marie.

They would then sexually abuse Anna Marie at any time from then on, by tying her to various items of furniture and forcing her into degrading acts. Fred would rape her regularly and then force her to do her chores while wearing a mini-skirt adorned with adult sexual devices.

When Anna Marie was 13, she was forced to become a sex worker in 'Rose's Room' with Rose watching every encounter with clients in case Anna Marie revealed her true age. Anna Marie was only one of the children – others would suffer even worse fates at the hands of Fred and Rose.

"I made you, I can do what I like with you." – Fred West, to his daughters.

They killed 12 young women between them, mostly their daughters, or hitchhikers who ended up at the house. In 1987, they killed their daughter, Heather West, and buried her under the patio of their garden. Fred even put a wooden table over her makeshift grave, a table where he would have family dinners outside in the Summer. The other children didn't know their sister was beneath them as they dined.

Uncovering the horrors

In 1973, a lodger at the house was tied up and subjected to abuse but she managed to escape while visiting a launderette. The West's were arrested for assault and rape but were released free of charge when the lodger refused to appear at the trial. The West's were let off with a £50 fine.

20 years later in 1993, the West's were arrested again when one of their daughters spoke out about the abuse but she too refused to testify in court. The West's were freed but their five remaining children were taken into foster care. While looking at the abuse case, investigators reopened the investigation into the disappearance of Heather West, who disappeared in 1987.

It was the reopening of the case that would ultimately lead investigators to uncover the horrors surrounding the West's and would lead to their arrest. It was the excavation of the patio after their arrest that led to multiple bodies and body parts being uncovered. The investigation found remains in the ground floor bathroom, multiple bodies in the cellar and a large number in the garden.

Each body had been heavily mutilated and had been subjected to extremely violent sexual abuse before their deaths. They found severed limbs, a skull, knives and various bondage materials. Bizarrely, every one of the human remains were missing some of their bones, most notably the phalange bones, which are the bones found in the fingers. Heather's remains were found in the same location. In total, the remains of nine victims were found at 25 Cromwell Street.

Initially, Rose denied murdering any victims and claimed to be a victim of Fred's but Fred confessed that she had helped in dismembering the corpses. In the instance of the death of one of their lodgers, Shirley Robinson, Rose had removed a foetus from her womb and put it in a plastic bag for burial in their garden.

Horrific legacy

Heather's death in 1987, was considered the West's final murder victim, and Fred would tell his surviving children – and sex slaves – that if they didn't follow orders that they would end up under the patio like Heather. At their trial, it materialised that Fred and Rose had made a pact where Fred would claim responsibility for all the murders to let Rose get away with it.

However, the investigation into the murders discovered that Rose was instrumental in some of them, and she was charged the same as Fred. On 30th June 1994, Fred was charged with 12 murders, and Rose with nine. Fred was also charged with the murder of Anne McFall, whose body had been found a couple of weeks earlier but not identified at the time.

On New Year's Day 1995, while awaiting trial, Fred killed himself in his prison cell by turning his blanket into a rope and hanging himself. In November 1995, Rose was convicted of ten murders and sentenced to life in prison without the possibility of parole. To this day, she continues to maintain her innocence.

During his interviews before his death, Fred West claimed to have killed 30 people, 20 with Rose, and was going to reveal the location of one body every year to investigators, claiming they were spread around Gloucester under paving stones. Since then, other crimes have been tentatively linked to him but have not been confirmed, including seven rapes in the 1970s. The fingers of his victims have never been found.

Rose West receives only one sole visitor; Anna Marie. In 1999, Anna Marie attempted suicide but was saved by a friend. One of the West's sons; Stephen, also attempted suicide in 2002. Later, in 2004, Stephen was jailed for having sex with a 14-year-old girl. It appears that the West's horrific legacy will ultimately continue to be felt.

The Shoe Fetish Slayer

The dark tale of a killer, whose overpowering fetish for women's shoes, led him to abduct and murder his victims while dressed as a woman – before committing unspeakable acts against their corpses.

Fetishes are common throughout the world, they can develop prior to adolescence but generally appear during puberty. Some psychologists believe that fetishism develops from early childhood experiences, normally with an object associated with sexual arousal or gratification.

These gratification objects are then connected with sexual maturity as a person ages. Fetishes also develop where some people seek gratification where they have no social sexual contacts in their lives.

This development of sexual fetish can be seen in the grim tale of Jerry Brudos, who went on to kill at least four women in Oregon between 1968 and 1969. His childhood tells us a little bit about how his fetish for shoes and women's clothes developed.

This fascination with women's shoes and their feet, would ultimately lead him to kill, in order to gratify himself and feed his fetish, where the desires were not being filled elsewhere. Jerry's life was bizarre, and so were the murders he committed.

A damaged brain

Born as Jerome Henry Brudos, in South Dakota in 1939, he was subjected to violent physical and emotional abuse by his mother, who wanted to have a daughter as her second child. She was so adamant about this that she was angry Jerry had turned out to be a boy.

From the age of five, after his mother moved him and his brother to Oregon, he developed his shoe fetish, and was once found in a junkyard playing with stiletto shoes while touching himself. He also stole women's underwear from washing lines and would wear them whenever he could.

At the age of seven, he attacked his female teacher and attempted to steal her shoes. This put him on the radar of a psychiatrist who was only granted minimal access to him, due to his mother blocking any therapy.

Around the same time, he was known to dress in women's clothes and he developed a female personality that would help him cope with the reality of his life. By his early teens, he was in and out of therapy and was becoming frustrated.

His frustration turned to anger, and from the age of 15, he began to stalk girls and women. Soon after, he began attacking them. He attacked at least three women by pushing them to the ground, choking them to unconsciousness, then eloping – with their shoes.

Overpowering fetish

At the age of 17, in Oregon, he dragged a young women into a remote area and beat her before threatening her with a knife. He ordered her to strip and perform sexual acts on him before escaping once again with her shoes. She was able to identify him and he was arrested shortly after.

He was admitted to a psychiatric hospital for almost a year. There, he was diagnosed with schizophrenia, and psychiatrists learned that his sexual fantasies revolved around his hatred towards his mother and females in general.

When he was released, he managed to live a relatively normal life for a number of years. He became an electrician, and at age 21, married a 17-year-old girl named Darcie. Together they would have two children, but soon enough, the gratification was fading and Jerry's fetish returned – ten-fold.

He began ordering Darcie to do her chores and housework naked – except for a pair of high heels. She obeyed her husband, and he was free to take photographs of her legs and shoes as she cleaned and cooked for him in the nude.

It remains unclear whether Darcie knew of his overpowering fetish beforehand and if she agreed to it or was forced. Still, his fetish became clearer when he became a transvestite and insisted on wearing Darcie's clothes around the house, while she was forced to wear none.

Then in 1968, age 29, the abuse from all those years ago, combined with the intense sexual desire for women's shoes, led Jerry to commit murder.

Opportunistic killing

The first murder came from an unfortunate circumstance, an opportunistic killing that set in place a turn of events leading to multiple murders. On 26th January 1968, 19-year-old encyclopedia salesperson Linda Slawson, made the mistake of knocking on Jerry's door.

Despite his mother and his children being in the house at the time, Jerry lured Linda to the basement where he knocked her out with a plank of wood. While she was unconscious, he strangled her to death.

After many hours of posing her corpse in sexual positions, and dressing her up in his own women's clothes, he sawed off her left foot. He wrapped it up and kept it in the basement freezer, before disposing of Linda's body in the nearby Willamette River.

The taste for murder had taken hold but he wanted his next victim to be as easy to lure as Linda. 10 months later, to the day, on 26th November, he spotted a broken-down car and offered to give the woman, 23-year-old Jan Whitney, a lift to his home.

Before he got home, he pulled over, strangled her and raped her corpse. He took the body home with him and hung her from a pulley in the garage for the next four days. He dressed the corpse in women's clothes, engaged in necrophilia, and photographed her.

Shortly before disposing of her body in the Willamette River, he cut off one of her breasts and made a plastic mould with it. He filled the mould with resin and used it as a paperweight.

Out of control

The investigation into the women's disappearances had already begun but with no bodies as evidence, the police were at a loss, leaving Jerry to continue killing. Realising other victims may not be so easy to come by, he resorted to forced abductions.

On 27th March 1969, while dressed as a woman, he abducted 18-year-old Karen Sprinker from a shopping centre car park. As with Whitney, he strangled her to death then hung her from a pulley in his garage, before engaging in necrophilia, and dressing her in various women's clothing. He also cut of both her breasts and made plastic moulds of them, before dumping her body in the same river.

The longer he got away with murder, the shorter the time between victims, and the desire to gratify himself intensified. On the 21st and 22nd of April, he attempted to abduct a 24-year-old woman and then a 15-year-old girl, but he failed in his attempts.

On the third day, 23rd April, he abducted 22-year-old Linda Salee from another shopping mall car park. He killed her and hung her from the same pulley in his garage. This time, he experimented on her, in a bizarre attempt to reanimate her corpse.

He ran multiple electrical currents through Linda's body, in an effort to restart her heart and brain. When this failed, he tied her body to an engine-part of a car and dumped her body in the Willamette River. Meanwhile, the net was closing in on Jerry.

Caught with photos

Two weeks later, a fisherman on his usual route along the Willamette, discovered two bodies in the river. Police quickly learned they were the bodies of Sprinker and Salee but due to the decomposition, there was minimal evidence to work with.

As they appealed for witnesses at a nearby university campus, some students came forward and told them of a creepy guy. They described Jerry in detail and told police he would act strange around some of the female students, while lusting over their shoes, and would sometimes be dressed as a woman.

One female student claimed that Jerry would constantly push her to go on a date with him but she refused. At one point, he had got hold of her phone number and would ring non-stop. Police then decided to put a sting operation in place.

They asked the student to phone Jerry and agree to go on a date with him. When Jerry arrived at the meeting point, police met him and interrogated him about the murders. Initially he gave a fake address but they quickly found out where he really lived.

Upon entering his garage, they found various pieces of evidence, including a cutting tool that had the same serrated edges as the tool used to cut the cords that were wrapped around the bodies. Then they found items of clothing – and shoes belonging to the victims.

And if that wasn't enough, they opened a drawer that contained hundreds of photos of Jerry posing with the corpses of three of his victims. He was arrested on the spot and immediately confessed.

In June 1969, Jerry was found guilty of three first-degree murders. He admitted to killing his first victim, Slawson, but because he had taken no photos with her, and her body was never recovered, prosecutors were not able to convict him.

However, there were photos of Slawson's left foot, but because there were no personal photographs of Slawson that showed her bare-footed, and with the foot dumped in the river too, there was no way to prove the foot belonged to Slawson.

The body of Whitney, his second victim, was found many months after Jerry's ultimate conviction of her murder. Darcie was arrested and questioned about any knowledge she had of the murders, but she told investigators that she was under the control of her husband and had to follow his orders.

With regards to the garage, Jerry had told her it was off-limits and she was not to enter without his permission. If she needed access, she had call him on the intercom. Unbeknownst to Darcie, the bodies of his victims might have been hanging in the garage, while she was doing her chores in the nude.

A witness came forward to claim she had seen both Jerry and Darcie carrying what looked like a mannequin into the garage one day, and later thought it could have been a body. But the evidence wasn't strong enough and Darcie was released. It is possible that she assisted her husband while under his control but it has never been proven.

Despite many appeals, and claims of having no memory of the attacks, Jerry was sentenced to life in prison, where he died of liver cancer in 2006, aged 67.

When his cell was cleaned out, guards found piles of women's shoe catalogues – that Jerry had been collecting to gratify his eternal fetish.

Killer in the Casino

A teenager killed a young girl in a casino restroom and pushed her body into the toilet, minutes after his friend walked in on the attack – and did nothing.

Casino's attract a wide range of people and can be fun and dangerous at the same time. Some put down their entire wage packet while others enjoy a small flutter like they would on a national lottery, if enjoyed the right way and within personal limits, a casino can be an experience like no other.

On 25th May 1997, Labor Day weekend, Leroy Iverson took his seven-year-old daughter, Sherrice, and her 14-year-old half-brother, Harold, to Primm, Nevada for a break away. Their mother, waitress Yolanda Manuel stayed at home in Los Angeles.

That evening, Leroy went to the Primadonna Resort and Casino to play slots and blackjack. Leroy wasn't addicted to gambling but enjoyed a bet every now and again, never normally winning big on the tables. Still, it was a pastime that suited him.

With no one to look after his children, Leroy took them to the casino with him. His son stayed with him most of the time but Sherrice was younger and wanted to play, as she had dressed up in a sailor outfit. On at least two occasions that evening, officials in the casino led Sherrice back to Leroy to look after.

But within minutes of being led back each time, Sherrice would run off to the video game section or play with adults who noticed her. One of those adults who took great interest in Sherrice was 18-year-old Jeremy Strohmeyer.

Little girl outfits

Born in 1978, Jeremy was raised in a damaging environment. His birth parents were both drug addicts and had a history of mental illness between them. His mother had been diagnosed with chronic schizophrenia and had been hospitalised at least 50 times.

Jeremy was taken into state care at a young age and adopted by new foster parents in Long Beach, California. They were never informed of why he had been removed from his parents, nor that they were suffering from combined drug and mental health issues.

As such, Jeremy had a predisposition for mental illness but it didn't excuse his future behaviour. Despite his parentage, he found it easy to get girlfriends but had a fetish for dressing them up in little girl outfits to satisfy his sexual appetite.

On 25th May, Jeremy and his 17-year-old friend, David Cash, and David's father, paid a visit to the Primadonna Resort and Casino, wearing baggy shorts and t-shirts. It wasn't long before Jeremy set his sights on Sherrice, taken by the young girl's playfulness and sailor costume.

At 4am, while Leroy was busy gambling, Jeremy asked Sherrice to play hide-and-seek with him. Later when detectives viewed the CCTV footage, it seemed entirely innocent; a young man playing with a young girl.

Nothing seemed overly untoward, until Jeremy told Sherrice that the only place she would be safe to hide was the ladies toilets. Not knowing what was to come, Sherrice ran away from Jeremy and hid where he had suggested. A few minutes later, making sure no one was looking, Jeremy followed her into the restroom.

Rape and murder

Still acting as though he was Sherrice's friend, he played a game of throwing wet paper towels at each other. But it was no game, Jeremy was luring her slowly to the disabled cubicle. He suddenly grabbed her and held his left hand over her mouth, while sexually groping her with his right.

At that moment, the door swung open and David walked in, wondering what his friend was up to. Jeremy shook his head at David as if telling him to keep it quiet and leave. David watched Jeremy groping Sherrice before he left them to it.

Jeremy then shut the door to the disabled cubicle and raped Sherrice. While she was being attacked, two women entered the restroom, so he began squeezing Sherrice's neck to keep her quiet. When the women left, he strangled her to death because she could identify him.

When he went to leave the cubicle, he noticed that she was still breathing, and wanted to make sure she was dead like they did in the movies. He reached an arm around her neck and squeezed hard in an attempt to break it.

When he heard a popping sound and her head twisted sharply, he knew the deed had been done. He then folded her body in half and squashed her feet first into the toilet bowl, before walking out as if nothing had happened.

Emotionless

Sherrice's body was found an hour later, the sight of which caused the local sheriff to call it the most gruesome case he had ever worked on. Video footage of Jeremy was put out to the press, and his college friends recognised him immediately, but David still hadn't said a word about what he had seen.

Jeremy was arrested as he attempted to flee through his backyard, and was quickly charged with first degree murder, kidnapping, rape, and sexual assault. When the arrest hit the news, commercial airlines refused to fly him back to Nevada and a private jet had to be arranged.

Due to his adopted family's wealth, Jeremy knew how to fly a plane, and instead of talking to officers about the murder, he joked about plane crashes and shared his knowledge about the airline industry. The officers escorting Jeremy referred to him as emotionless and nonchalant about the murder he had committed.

At the trial, Jeremy's defence attempted to place the blame on David, who had turned witness for the prosecution. They claimed David was the real murderer, and that Jeremy was high on drugs at the time, both of which were never proven.

It was discovered that Jeremy's biological father was in prison for drug and assault offences and his biological mother had been admitted to a long-stay psychiatric hospital, which the defence attempted to use as a reason for Jeremy's behaviour.

Not willing to risk a death sentence, Jeremy pleaded guilty to first-degree murder, first-degree kidnapping, and two separate sexual assaults on a minor. In September 1998, he was sentenced to life imprisonment without the possibility of parole. But the furore had only just begun.

The Bad Samaritan

The public were outraged that Jeremy was not sentenced to death despite pleading guilty. During the pre-trial, Jeremy insinuated he had killed Sherrice because she was black, and because he was white he would be able to get away with it, which led to death sentence campaigns rising up around the country.

For his own protection at the maximum security Ely State Prison, Jeremy was moved to a special isolated cell away from the general population, as rumours were flying around that some inmates wanted their own revenge for the crime he had committed.

Sherrice's family suggested that David be charged as an accessory to the murder as he was seen going into the ladies restroom after Jeremy. But there was no evidence to suggest he had taken part in the murder, and his deal with the prosecution to turn witness meant he couldn't be charged.

After a series of interviews in the press, where David confessed he wasn't going to lose any sleep after Sherrice's death and that he was going to make money off the back of the trial, he was referred to as The Bad Samaritan.

Human responsibility

David never expressed remorse over what happened but his inability to stop his friend attacking a young girl became a cause of concern. Campaigns were created to have him removed from his university but they fell on deaf ears because the truth was that David hadn't committed a crime, at least not a criminal one.

There is no general law in the United States or United Kingdom that requires people to report a crime or stop a crime in progress. However, Nevada later passed a bill that required people to report a crime where a person under the age of 18 is being sexually or physically abused. A similar law was passed in California but for those under the age of 14.

Interfering in a crime is considered a moral judgement personal to the witness in question. The new laws meant that if the incident happened again then David could have been charged with not reporting the crime. To this day, the law remains controversial and is rarely invoked.

Despite numerous appeals, Jeremy remains incarcerated but was moved to a medium security prison. His adoptive parents attempted to sue Los Angeles social workers for withholding the drug and mental health issues of his birth parents. They failed but remain supportive of their adopted son.

Many people will never be confronted with witnessing a crime such as the Sherrice rape and murder and will never have to face the decision of whether or not to intervene. But the hope remains that moral judgement and human responsibility may outweigh the guilt of simply letting it go.

Babes in the Ditch Murderer

Raymond Morris, known as the A34 Killer, Babes in the Ditch murderer, or Monster of Cannock Chase, killed three girls and abused many more, leading to one of the largest manhunts in British history.

Though the Moors Murders are well known in the country today, when Ian Brady and Myra Hindley killed five children between 1963 and 1965, the Cannock Chase murders were as infamous in the latter half of the 1960s.

Factory worker Raymond Leslie Morris killed at least three young girls between 1965 and 1967, virtually picking up where the Moors Murderers had left off. Also known as the A34 Killer, the Babes in the Ditch murderer, or The Monster of Cannock Chase, Morris was the subject of one of the largest manhunts in British history.

The murders took place in and around the nature park of Cannock Chase in Staffordshire, home to sprawling forests and plentiful hiking trails. Cannock Chase also played an important part in the First World War, where two large military training camps were built due to its inland location.

Yet it is more known for the location where the bodies of three young girls between the ages of 5 and 7 were found. Over the years, Morris has been linked to other attempted murders and sexual assaults, making him one of the most prolific child killers in British history.

The tale of the Cannock Chase Murderer began with a brutal attack on nine-year-old Julie Taylor. As she walked home in the late evening of 2nd December 1964, a car pulled up alongside her, and inside was a man calling himself Uncle Len, claiming to be a friend of Julie's mother.

She was lured into his car on the pretence that they had to go and pick up Christmas presents from Julie's auntie. Julie agreed but became nervous when they drove past her auntie's house, and onwards to the mining village of Bentley where they parked up near an old mining waste ground. It was there that Uncle Len made his true intentions known.

Julie was raped multiple times, abused, tortured, and strangled. She was then thrown from the car into a nearby ditch. As luck would have it, less than an hour later, a passing cyclist heard Julie's whimpers and discovered her half-naked and damaged body.

Had the cyclist not found her, then she most certainly would have died from her wounds, which were extensive. She had suffered major internal injuries and was rushed to the hospital covered in blood and bruises.

Unknown to the area at the time, Raymond Leslie Morris had begun his campaign of abuse and violence and was later linked to Julie's attack. It appeared that Uncle Len was Morris, and Julie was his first known victim.

Almost a year later, in Aston, on 8th September 1965, six-year-old Margaret Reynolds disappeared on her way back to school after lunch. The route she had taken was short and obvious, difficult for someone to lose their way. At some point on the track, she vanished.

Despite a large investigation involving 160 police officers and 25,000 interviews, no trace of her was found. The locals were so invested in the disappearance that every single house was searched within an eight mile radius of the school but to no avail, she had simply disappeared.

In the weeks before Julie's disappearance, police received reports of a single white man driving around and asking young girls to get into his car. Some had been sexually assaulted but managed to get away or were let go by the man after he had penetrated them with his fingers. The man was never found but was later suspected to be Morris.

Five days after Christmas, in the same year, five-year-old Diana Tift vanished as she walked home alone from her grandmother's home in the early afternoon. Diana never made it home and was reported missing almost immediately.

Already disturbed by Margaret's disappearance three months earlier, local residents amassed a 2,000-strong search team to look for her, with various rewards popping up. As they searched for Diana, the realisation dawned that a child abductor was in their midst and had been responsible for both girls disappearances.

Police immediately made the connection to the 1964 attack on Julie Taylor and moved the search towards the Cannock Chase area of natural beauty. An additional 500 officers from the West Midlands region were put on the case to find the missing girls.

They searched gardens, sheds, greenhouses, lakes, rivers, ponds, and wooded areas but there was no sign of Diana or Margaret. Then two weeks later on 12th January 1966, a man hunting rabbits at Mansty Gully on Cannock Chase made a gruesome discovery.

The man had stumbled upon the half-naked body of Diana, somewhat hidden in the undergrowth of a drainage ditch, less than half a mile from the main A34 road. As the man raised the alarm he noticed something else further up the ditch but wasn't quite sure what he was looking at.

What appeared to be a mass of leaves and twigs, turned out to be the decomposed nude body of Margaret Reynolds. It appeared the girl's killer had used the same dumping ground to hide his crimes and in the case of Margaret had somewhat succeeded, as due to the decomposition, pathologists were unable to confirm a cause of death.

Diana had been raped and suffocated with her own coat when the killer covered her nose and mouth. Police were forced to put out a press release stating that they were hunting a dangerous child killer who may strike again. And in that degree, they were right, as Morris could not contain his dark desires longer than a few months.

Despite the massive nationwide manhunt for the killer of the two girls, it would be almost two years before Morris was finally caught but in that time he was free to attack many more. At one point police suspected the rabbit hunter to be the killer as he had a violent past but he was ruled out due to early forensic testing.

On 14th August 1966, 10-year-old Jane Taylor was abducted while riding her bike in the Cheshire village or Mobberley, 50 miles away from Cannock Chase. Police linked her disappearance to the murders around Cannock Chase but no trace of her was found at the time and having the same surname as Julie Taylor was only a coincidence.

A year-and-a-half after the bodies of Diana and Margaret had been found, the police search and investigation had dwindled due to the lack of information that was coming in. There were fewer avenues to pursue and lesser leads.

They resorted to preparing for the next incident and put a plan in place to have roadblocks set up within 20 minutes of a reported abduction. The plan of waiting for another abduction sent the public into a panic and accusations of shoddy police work were thrown around in the press.

Then, on 19th August 1967, just as the cases were going cold, seven-year-old Christine Darby was abducted as she played with friends in Caldmore, Walsall, ten miles from Cannock Chase. The driver asked for directions but lured Christine into the car as he feigned being confused about where to go.

Her friends raised the alarm and the police were called almost immediately. The plan of implementing roadblocks was put into place and a circle was drawn around Walsall to prevent the car, considered to be grey by Christine's friends, from getting past them.

The plan failed and suddenly they had another missing young girl on their hands, and an angry public protesting against them. Another large search was put together to find Christine in the hope she may still be alive somewhere.

Her friends insisted the man spoke with a local accent and drove a grey car, backing up initial police belief's that they were dealing with a local man close to Cannock Chase. Three hundred officers and some off-duty soldiers began the arduous task of searching the large nature park.

Three days later on 22nd August, one of the soldiers stumbled across Christine's nude body, barely hidden in the undergrowth of a wooded patch. The body was found less than a mile from the location of Diana and Margaret.

She was found spreadeagled on her back with blood soaked into the ground beneath her. Her tongue protruding from her mouth confirmed she had been suffocated to death. She had been raped and murdered in the very location she had been found.

As the investigation went into overdrive, police realised they were dealing with a serial killer, with a weakness for young girls. All three of the murdered girls lived within 17 miles of each other, and close to the A34 road, leading to some reporters calling them the A34 Murders.

As police had found the body shortly after death, the area was descended upon by forensic experts and detectives. They found tyre tracks leading in and out of the wooded area, clearly made by the killer due to where the tracks had stopped.

In the week that followed, over 600 vehicles were traced and ultimately ruled out of the investigation. Two hikers in Cannock Chase remembered seeing a grey vehicle parked in the woods and noted a man with dark hair nearby. All reports suggested the vehicle was a grey Austin A55 or A60.

In the months that followed, a special incident room was set up to track 23,000 owners of Austin vehicles in the Midlands, involving 200 officers and a purpose built evidence storage unit. The search expanded to interview 44,000 owners of Austin vehicles outside the Midlands.

Using witness accounts, and for the first time in British history, police created a colour facial composite of the man they suspected was the killer. It ended up being published on the front pages of many national British newspapers.

For the next year, police interviewed several thousand suspects but nothing came of it. They set up an initiative to interview every man in the county but it failed due to the massive scale of the operation. Once again, the killer had escaped capture – until the next abduction was rumbled.

On 4th November 1968, 10-year-old Margaret Aulton was playing near the side of a road throwing wood onto an unlit bonfire in preparation for Guy Fawkes night the next day, when a car pulled up next to her, and the man asked if she would like some free fireworks.

When Aulton refused, the man tried to forcibly drag her into the car but she managed to break free and run away. An 18-year-old named Wendy Lane was exiting a chip shop opposite when she witnessed the attempted abduction and ran towards the car, causing the man to drive off at high speed.

Fortunately, Aulton was not abducted, and more fortunately, Lane managed to note down the number plate, colour, and make of car; a green

Ford Corsair. Police were led to 39-year-old Raymond Leslie Morris who lived in a council estate block – directly opposite Walsall police station.

It turned out that police had already interviewed him four times relating to the abductions and murders but his wife had given an alibi each time. On 15th November, Morris was arrested and charged with the murder of Christine Darby. His wife confirmed she had given a false alibi based on what Morris had told her.

To back up the charge, police executed a warrant on Morris's house and found a box full of homemade child pornography, most of whom involved the same girl, later discovered to be his five-year-old niece. He was originally charged with the murder of Christine Darby due to a witness placing him at the scene, the attempted abduction of Margaret Aulton, and a charge of indecent assault against his niece.

He pleaded guilty to abusing his niece but innocent to any connection with the murders and abductions, something he would protest until the end of his days. The trial was built on the basis of two eye-witness statements claiming that Morris was the man they'd seen in the car or near the crime scene.

There was no forensic evidence put forward to prove Morris was the killer. Circumstantial evidence including petrol station receipts, employment clocking-off cards, and timelines when he wasn't with his family, were seemingly enough to convict him on.

On 18th February 1969, Morris was found guilty of the murder of Christine, the attempted abduction of Aulton, and the abuse of his niece, leading to a life sentence. But who was Morris? Why had he killed the girls? And was he truly the culprit?

Morris had lived in Walsall all his life and was known to be sexually dominant, violent to his previous partners, and had a high level of intelligence. In 1966, he was arrested while taking photographs of two underage girls who he had lured to his council flat – something the police investigation never connected to the later murders. He was let go due to no evidence found in the flat.

It was clear that Morris had a dark taste for young girls, whom he could control and exert dominance over. That he was never considered a strong suspect was damaging to the police investigation, and many considered his wife should have been charged with providing a false alibi.

Despite never being charged with the murders of Diana Tift and Margaret Reynolds, or the disappearance of Jane Taylor, the cases were closed as Morris fitted the profile, along with the fact that Christine's body was found near the other two girls, despite no evidence suggesting it was Morris.

The families of the dead and missing hold strong beliefs that Morris was the perpetrator, along with the fact that the murders and abductions stopped in the area after his arrest.

But in 2010, after 41 years in prison, Morris was granted a review in a bid to overturn his conviction as there was no forensic evidence to conclude he had killed Christine, only circumstantial and via two witnesses. Incidentally, if the trial had been carried out today, the evidence would not have been enough to convict him of the murder.

Incidentally, Morris never confessed and maintained his innocence right up until his death of leukaemia in 2014, having spent 45 years in prison. Among his last words were, *'I didn't do it, and I hope that someone will listen.'*

If not Morris then who? The disappearance of 10-year-old Jane Taylor 50 miles away from Cannock Chase ended when her skeletal remains were found in 1972 in North Wales, six years after her disappearance.

She had been murdered by a man named William Ian Copeland, who confessed to another inmate while he was in jail on unrelated charges. Copeland was charged and convicted of her murder in 1975. Like Morris's trial, the conviction was based on circumstantial evidence but in that instance, Copeland confessed.

There are some who suspect that Copeland may have had a hand in the murders of Margaret and Diana, and even Christine but he was already in prison for two of them and was not known to live in the area at the time.

It seems unusual that the cases of Margaret and Diana were never tried in a court of law, and the only assumption one can make is that if they had done then the minimal evidence against Morris would have seen him walk free.

That Morris didn't confess to Christine's murder was perhaps the last bit of control he had left, hoping that one day he would be retried and found innocent, free to rape and kill again. Morris abused many girls including his own niece, had a predilection for child pornography, and even took pictures of underage girls in his flat.

Morris killed three young girls and dumped their bodies in Cannock Chase, their dignity wrecked, ripped away by a monster hiding in plain sight. If he had not been caught then it's likely that the Monster of Cannock Chase would have continued to kill, leaving families destroyed in his wake.

A Victorian Murder

In Victorian London, a lady of the night was found in her room with her throat slashed, and the door locked from the outside. Read the story of one of the oldest unsolved murders in London.

Great Coram Street, now simply Coram Street, is located one block away from Russell Square Tube Station, in the Bloomsbury area of London. It's an area rich with hotels, hostels, and self-catering apartments, a feature carried over from Victorian times.

On Christmas afternoon, 1872, the landlady of lodgings in Great Coram Street, became concerned when one of her tenants didn't return her calls. She had the door to the room broken down by some burly men, who were met with a horrific sight.

Laying in her bed with her face turned to the ceiling, was 27-year-old penniless London prostitute and wannabe actress, Harriet Buswell. Her throat had been cut from ear to ear, and her bedclothes were stained with blood.

Harriet's death remains one of the oldest unsolved murders in London. Preceding Jack the Ripper by 16 years, the Great Coram Street Murder continues to fascinate both true crime enthusiasts, and those who believe the Ripper may have been around a little earlier.

The Lost Alhambra

Harriet was working at one of the local theatres in London, as a member of the 'corps de ballet', a background dancer, but her dream was to be an actress. Because the theatre paid her a pittance, she resorted to prostitution to pay for her day to day living.

For four weeks prior to her murder, she had managed to secure lodgings with landlady Mrs. Wright at 12 Great Coram Street. Harriet had left her previous landlady of two years for reasons unknown and asked Mrs. Wright if she could have a room for at least a week.

After which, she requested to have an apartment but Mrs. Wright stated she only let out apartments to men. Mrs. Wright was unaware that Harriet would be using the room for nightly encounters with men paying for her services.

On Christmas Eve, Harriet left the lodgings to visit the Alhambra Theatre Bar in Leicester Square, she was wearing a black silk dress, black velvet jacket, and a dark green brigand hat with a red feather. The Alhambra was one of the few bars in London that accepted women without the escort of a man. Once described as the '*greatest place of infamy in all London.*'

The theatre bar burned down in 1882 and was rebuilt but was said to be cursed by debauchery. It was demolished and rebuilt again as the Odeon Cinema. Today, a cocktail bar next to the Odeon, called the Lost Alhambra, has been resurrected, though less infamous than its Victorian roots.

Harriet would frequent the Alhambra on numerous occasions and it became a place to pick up well-to-do men, and some less upstanding men. That night, she caught an omnibus – a horse drawn bus – with two of the barmaids from the Alhambra, along with an unidentified male friend.

The omnibus took them all from Piccadilly Circus to Russell Square, where Harriet stepped off with her male friend. She returned to her lodgings in the late of the night and told Mrs. Wright that she had a gentleman with her.

Harriet had borrowed some money from another tenant to pay her rent and she gave Mrs. Wright a half-sovereign from which to take her rent for the following week. After getting back one shilling, she retreated to her room where the male friend was waiting – and was never seen alive again.

Large enough to put a man's fist in

At 3pm on Christmas afternoon, police were called to Harriet's room, and they reported one of the most horrific crimes they had seen until then. Detective Superintendent Thomson relayed their initial findings to the press:

"The murderer stabbed the poor girl under the left ear, and there is another wound on the left of the wind-pipe large enough to put a man's fist in. The object of the murderer was evidently to possess himself of what trinkets and money the girl possessed, for earrings which she had borrowed to wear were not to be found; and a purse into which she was seen to put the shilling change was also missing."

Spots of blood were found in various places around the room, which led police to believe the killer must have been splattered with Harriet's blood. Her body was taken to St. Giles's Workhouse morgue, and was identified by her brother, who travelled from their home county of Berkshire.

Police tracked down the two barmaids who said that Harriet was in the company of a German-speaking man of high calibre. A fruit shop owner came forward to say he had seen Harriet enter his shop with the man but suspected nothing to be wrong at the time.

The investigation agreed the man must have had blood on his clothing, as the wounds Harriet had received would have sprayed blood in every direction. There were bloodstains in the sink where the killer would have washed his hands.

He also took the time to lock the door to the room behind him as he exited and took the key with him. He was heard by other tenants leaving the building in the early hours of Christmas morning. Descriptions of the man were amalgamated and released to the press and public.

"He is about 23 years of age, 5ft. 9in. high, with neither beard, whiskers, nor moustache, but not having shaved for two or three days, his beard when grown would be rather dark. He has a swarthy complexion, and blotches or pimples on his face. He was dressed in dark clothes and

wore a dark brown overcoat down to the knees, billycock hat, and rather heavy boots."

The Wangerland

Two days later, reports were spreading of a male passenger who fitted the description, being spotted at Harwich port, ready to board the Great Eastern route ferry to Rotterdam in the Netherlands. But police claimed the killer would not have got there in time as his description was sent to the ports as soon as it had been released.

Except, there was a ship in Ramsgate Harbour that flew a German flag, and knowing they were looking for a German-speaking man, police descended on the ship. The Wangerland was a German emigrant ship that was undergoing repairs at the harbour.

Due to the brutality of the murder, the case had spread around England like wildfire, and it became the talk of the country. Knowing they had to find a suspect soon, the police put all their efforts into the German link.

They initially suspected a chemist from the ship named Carl Wohllebe but they needed to have him identified by the witnesses. To fill out the line-up, the police picked some other Germans at random from the ship and put them together.

As the revolving door of witnesses were shown the line-up of Germans, the police were surprised to see that no-one picked Carl. Instead, some pointed the finger to the ship's chaplain, Dr. Gottfried Hessel, as he slightly resembled the killer. Many more ruled him out completely.

But the police needed a suspect. They learned that Hessel had been in London from 23rd December and had a history of fraud and financial crime – which was enough. On 21st January 1873, Hessel appeared in court, charged with Harriet's wilful murder.

It didn't quite go the way police had intended it too. For starters, Hessel had been ill with bronchitis at the time of the murder and remained in his own hotel room over Christmas. His illness was backed up by his wife and many hotel workers who confirmed he was room-bound, thus giving him an alibi.

The magistrates threw out the case on the basis of the alibis and found Hessel innocent of any wrongdoing, even compensating him for wrongful arrest. The police couldn't see past their belief that the killer was Hessel, and in doing so, may have given time for the real killer to get away.

A Victorian mystery

Though policing was not to the standard it is in today's world, the murder of Harriet Buswell created quite the furore in Victorian London, and every effort was made to catch the killer. It is possible that some witnesses confused German with any other foreign language.

London was the epicentre of 19th Century multiculturalism, and people from all over the world were roaming the streets, looking for their piece of the pie in business or in leisure – or in something darker.

Something horrific occurred at that rundown lodge-house on Great Coram Street over Christmas in 1872. A murder that has remained unsolved for 140 years, despite various attempts to reach into the past and dig for unseen clues.

The spirit of Christmas was strong in London that year, with families coming together to celebrate. But another spirit had come to London at the same time to wreak death and bloody murder on an unsuspecting young woman, who simply aspired to be something greater than the life she was dealt.

It remains unlikely that Hessel was the killer, the alibis were too strong, and his illness too prevalent to have seen him roam the cold streets and decadent bars. The man Harriet brought back to her room may not have been the killer, and someone else may have entered after the man had left.

What really happened to Harriet that night remains a mystery, beyond the evidence of the murder. We may never know who or what violently took her life that Christmas but it appears that someone got away with murder.

The ghost of Harriet was said to have haunted the lodgings for decades afterwards, until the street was rebuilt following the two world wars. But even today, as the bells chime across London, and families celebrate Christmas, the echoes of Harriet's death remain.

Thames Torso Murders

In Victorian London, the dismembered bodies of eight women turned up across the city, during the same period when Jack the Ripper was active.

Jack the Ripper is without doubt the most famous unidentified serial killer in history. He terrorised London throughout 1888, claiming at least five victims by mutilating their bodies, before disappearing into the annals of true crime history.

Wherever you stand, or whoever you may have identified as the ripper, it will never be solved – millions have tried. And yet, the stories, books, articles and websites surround Jack continue to grow. This story is not about Jack the Ripper, but he is very much a part of its framework.

From 1873 to 1889, the dismembered bodies of eight females were found across London. Only one has ever been identified, and their killer or killers have never been found. Though many researchers associate four bodies with the so-called Thames Torso Murders, there were an additional four.

The first was known as the Battersea Mystery, when on 5th September 1873, the left torso of an unidentified female was found by police near Battersea pier. Over the course of the following two days, the rest of the woman's body parts were discovered.

The right side of the torso was found, along with a right breast, a forearm, a pelvis, and a head that had been skinned and scalped. On the second day, the woman's face and scalp were floating in the water at the Limehouse Basin but were missing the nose and chin.

By the end of the day, police surgeon Thomas Bond had reconstructed a near-complete corpse of a female. They displayed the corpse to the public in the hopes someone might recognise her. The hurriedly stitched together body was viewed by hundreds of people, but the mystery was just beginning.

Just over two weeks later, no identity was made, and the remains were buried at Battersea cemetery.

Bond concluded the body had not been hacked by a madman but by someone with competent medical skills.

The joints had been opened up, the bones had been perfectly separated, and the hip and shoulders had been sawn through with impeccable precision. Cause of death was confirmed to have been blunt force trauma to the head.

A year later, in June 1874, the dismembered body of another female was found on the banks of the River Thames at Putney. Her head, hands, and feet were missing. No cause of death was ascertained but her death was listed as an unsolved murder.

The remains had been treated with lime, which is now known to be highly effective in preventing decay and protecting the body rather than destroying it. Back in Victorian times, there were articles suggesting that lime could increase the speed of the body's decay.

The female was never identified, and a jury returned a verdict of wilful murder against some person or persons unknown, meaning the case remained unsolved. Both the 1873 and 1874 women were listed as unsolved murders.

For a decade, the stories of the two victims disappeared from public knowledge until October 1884, when the Times newspaper reported on a new discovery. A woman's skull and thighbone were found in Tottenham Court Road, while at the same time, the same woman's arm was found in Bedford Square.

The arm had a tattoo on it which could have helped identify the victim but there was no record of the tattoo anywhere. In Victorian London, a tattoo on a female sometimes meant that she was a sex worker.

Five days later, a constable was on duty in Fitzroy Square near the West End, when he found a large paper parcel on the side of the small park. He opened it to find a section of a female torso. The parcel had been discarded by the killer when the police shift change happened, which meant the killer knew the police routines.

An inquest held in November concluded the body parts had come from the same female, and like the two previous bodies ten years earlier, had been skilfully dissected by someone with professional medical knowledge.

In December 1884, another parcel was found in the resident's garden at Mornington Crescent, close to Camden. It contained the bones of two arms and two feet. The body parts belonged to a different female, making it the second to be found in a matter of months, and the fourth in the ever-growing list of mystery torsos appearing across London.

The Mornington Crescent bones were stored at St. Pancras Mortuary for a short period and later buried at an unnamed cemetery. The packaging used to wrap both women's remains were similar, meaning the same killer or killers had dissected and disposed of the bodies.

Colloquially referred to as the Thames Torso Murders, the next four bodies turned up near the Thames and across central London from 1887 to 1889. Though many researchers point to these four as the official torso murders, the previously mentioned discoveries will forever be linked to them, making eight in total.

In May 1887, body parts began washing up on the River Thames. In the river near Rainham, construction workers found a package that contained the torso of a female. From then until June, various body parts of the same female were discovered around the same area.

No head or the upper part of the chest were found. Like the previous women, the investigation concluded the body had not been dissected for medical purposes. All the parts found in Rainham belonged to the same female.

An inquiry could not ascertain a cause of death and returned a verdict of 'found dead.' And like the others, she remained unidentified. Her death became known as the Rainham Mystery.

Over a year later on 11th September 1888, a right arm and shoulder were found on the bank of the Thames in Pimlico, in a case known as the Whitehall Mystery. A few weeks later on 2nd October, a construction worker found a parcel containing further human remains.

Curiously, the worker was part of the construction team working on the Metropolitan Police's new headquarters, which would soon be known to the world as New Scotland Yard. The parcel was found in a newly-built vault, and the killer had placed the parcel in there just a few days before its discovery.

Police surgeon Thomas Bond, who had worked on the 1873 body, confirmed that the body parts belonged to the same female. On 17th October, a reporter found a left leg close to the construction site, which also belonged to the same female.

Around the same time, the Jack the Ripper murders had begun, leading to instant speculation that 'Jack' was responsible for the torso murders. However, there was no obvious connection between the killings.

The torso discoveries and the ripper killings were very different in nature. Where Jack the Ripper mutilated his victims, the torso killer was seemingly dismembering the bodies to hide either his identity or the identity of the victims.

There has long been speculation that the torso killer was teasing the police by leaving many of the body parts where they would be found – even at the New Scotland Yard construction site. The identities of the Rainham and Whitehall victims remain a mystery.

There was no respite in the discoveries, as on 4th June 1889, the torso of another female was discovered in the Thames, near to Battersea. And in a chilling similarity to the Battersea victim of 1873, additional body parts were found in the Limehouse Basin and around the same area.

Once again, an investigation into the remains concluded that the same level of surgical skill had been used to dismember the victim, but it had not been carried out for medical purposes. The female had only been dead for approximately 48 hours before her body parts were found.

Unlike the other discoveries, and due to the minimal time between death and discovery, the victim's identity was uncovered. When her arm was found, there was a garment with the name 'L.E. Fisher embroidered into it.

This along with a large scar on her wrist, and the fact she was discovered to be eight months pregnant, helped her to be identified as 24-year-old homeless sex worker Elizabeth Jackson, despite her head not being found.

Though Jack the Ripper's reign had come to an end half a year earlier, the press believed the ripper was back. Elizabeth's arm was thrown over a private wall and discovered on the grounds of the Mary Shelley estate, the same Mary Shelley who wrote Frankenstein in 1818, and died in 1951.

It was perhaps no coincidence that the killer was taunting police by leaving a body part on the estate of the author who wrote a book about piecing body parts back together. Once again, an enquiry into Elizabeth's death concluded she had been murdered, like the others.

On 10th September 1889, a police constable found the headless and legless torso of another unidentified woman under a railway arch at Pinchin Street in Whitechapel. As Jack the Ripper's murders had taken place in and around Whitechapel, the discovery was instantly linked to the ripper in the press.

An investigation carried out on the body showed that the victim had been beaten to death and her abdomen had been mutilated. The mutilation led to speculation it was the ripper's final victim, but the dismemberment and lack of genital mutilation meant it did not fit the same modus operandi.

A large search of the surrounding areas was carried out but no other body parts belonging to the woman were found. Despite many people coming forward claiming to know who the victim was, her identity, like most of the others, remains unknown.

The four murders that took place from 1887 to 1889, were linked to an unidentified serial killer simply known as the torso killer. The Thames Torso Murders remain unsolved and only one of the official four victims remains identified.

As time passed and the cases went cold, the four discoveries from 1873 to 1874 were added to the list, as the similarity between them was difficult to ignore. There were a possible eight victims of the London torso killer, with none of the cases ever being solved.

Modern researchers and Jack the Ripper experts have discounted his connection to the torso killings. Because the MO was so different. It meant that at least two unidentified serial killers were operating in Victorian London around the same time.

Some writers point to medical establishments using illegal techniques to abduct women and experiment on their bodies. However, all the victims of the torso mysteries showed no signs of experimentation and were not dissected by a skilled surgeon but by someone with some knowledge of dismemberment.

It could point to a butcher or knacker as the suspect. A knacker is someone who disposes of dead or unwanted animals not fit for human consumption. But the most unusual aspect of the torso mysteries is the very public locations the body parts were found.

It was as if the killer was taunting police by leaving parcels of body parts on their known routes, at the site of the new police headquarters, and even throwing an arm over the private wall of the Mary Shelley estate.

Unlike Jack the Ripper, there is no long speculative list of suspects, and only one of the eight victims was ever identified. As bad as Jack the Ripper was, there seems to have been another horrific serial killer, hiding in the shadows of Victorian London, who was perhaps even worse.

Axeman of New Orleans

A mystery serial killer with a penchant for axes and bloody murder, threatened to kill more people on a specific date – unless he heard jazz music echoing throughout the city.

On 13th March 1919, an unidentified serial killer sent a letter to the newspapers of New Orleans claiming that on 19th March, he would kill again. However, he would spare any people and locations where a jazz band was playing.

"Now, to be exact, at 12:15 (earthly time) on next Tuesday night, I am going to pass over New Orleans. In my infinite mercy, I am going to make a little proposition to you people. Here it is:

"I am very fond of jazz music, and I swear by all the devils in the nether regions that every person shall be spared in whose home a jazz band is in full swing at the time I have just mentioned. If everyone has a jazz band going, well, then, so much the better for you people. One thing is certain and that is that some of your people who do not jazz it out on that specific Tuesday night (if there be any) will get the axe."

On the night of the 19th, New Orleans dropped into forced-party mode. Dance halls were packed with jazz bands, house parties were in full effect with jazz music blaring out of the windows, and people were playing jazz in the streets. No one was murdered that night.

But from May 1918 to October 1919, six people, mostly Italian immigrants or Italian-Americans were killed with an axe. The killer has never been identified and the case remains unsolved to this day.

Post-Civil War New Orleans was changing rapidly, the plantations had been broken up and thousands of African-Americans had poured into the city, becoming one of the most multi-cultural places in America for a time.

Jazz was the new music of the era, representing multiculturalism in the large Louisiana city. Young people especially were being drawn to jazz and blues music, which fought against the tide of segregation and separatism. It became a city very much defined by Jazz.

By the early 20th Century, the French Quarter had become the Italian neighbourhood, with so many Italians becoming resident in the area that it was referred to as *Little Palermo*. Being an Italian grocer in New Orleans was seen as the top of the career chain.

The first known victims of the Axeman fell on 23rd May 1918, when Italian grocer Joseph Maggio and his wife Catherine were sleeping in their home above their store and bar. The Axeman broke in through an upstairs window, sliced their necks with a razor, then bashed their heads in with an axe. Catherine's neck was sliced so deeply, her head was partially severed.

Investigators found the bloody clothes of the killer, as he had changed into a set of new ones before he left the Maggio residence. No money or belongings were taken. Joseph's brother was a suspect but other witnesses claimed to have seen a different man lurking in the shadows the same night.

"When I see fit, I shall come and claim other victims. I alone know whom they shall be. I shall leave no clue except my bloody axe, besmeared with blood and brains of he, whom I have sent below to keep me company."

One month later, on 27th June, Louis Besumer and his mistress Harriet Lowe were attacked in the living quarters of their grocery shop. Both were struck in the head multiple times and left in a bloody pool near their bed. The axe was found in the bathtub.

Both Besumer and Lowe survived the attack. Lowe was paralysed but a month later claimed it was Besumer who had attacked her, despite police arresting a black man named Lewis Oubicon who Lowe claimed had been in the shop the same day.

Due to Lowe's state of confusion before her death two months later, both men were later acquitted. It remains unclear how one could chop their own head with an axe.

The attacks and murders continued right through the Winter, and at each crime scene, investigators were led to different people as the suspect. But in each case, as with the Besumer and Lowe attack, the suspects were not involved.

"They have never caught me and they never will. They have never seen me, for I am invisible, even as the ether that surrounds your earth. I am not a human being, but a spirit and a demon from the hottest hell. I am what you Orleanians and your foolish police call the Axeman.

"If you wish you may tell the police to be careful not to rile me. Of course, I am a reasonable spirit. I take no offense at

the way they have conducted their investigations in the past. In fact, they have been so utterly stupid as to not only amuse me, but His Satanic Majesty, Francis Josef, etc.

Several attacks that didn't target Italians were also thought to be the work of the Axeman but were never proven. The city of New Orleans was put on high alert and the people were becoming terrified. The Axeman, in his letter, referred to the people as esteemed mortals.

The Italian immigrant community were especially terrified and were known to have stayed up at night to guard their families, as the police had no leads to go on.

On 9th March 1919, the Axeman visited the neighbouring city of Gretna, attacking Charlie Cortimiglia and his wife, Rosie, and killing their two-year-old daughter. Under pressure from the public, the police arrested and charged the Cortimiglia's elderly next door neighbour and his 17-year-old son.

The pair were tried for murder and sentenced to death, after police forced Rosie to say the pair were responsible for the murder. An intervention from the New Orleans police chief and a retraction of Rosie's statement led to the men's acquittal.

"But tell them to beware. Let them not try to discover what I am, for it were better that they were never born than to

incur the wrath of the Axeman. I don't think there is any need of such a warning, for I feel sure the police will always dodge me, as they have in the past. They are wise and know how to keep away from all harm."

An extortion crime known as the Black Hand existed in America from the mid-18th Century to the early 20th, specifically targeting Italian businesses. As with other types of extortion, the victims were threatened with violence if money wasn't paid for whatever reason suited that criminal. Generally, the Black Hand afforded protection to arriving immigrants.

At the time, the Italian community rarely spoke up about such occurrences and the theory propagated among early 20th Century New Orleanians. It was suggested the Axeman was a hitman for the Black Hand or made up of various people associated with extorting Italian businesses.

Another theory at the time was a *'Jack the Ripper'* killer, a fiend in the night who constantly had the urge to kill and took it out on his victims. Curious then that the Axeman only targeted Italians. But then, Jack the Ripper had only targeted prostitutes.

"Undoubtedly, you Orleanians think of me as a most horrible murderer, which I am, but I could be much worse if I wanted to. If I wished, I could pay a visit to your city every night. At will, I could slay thousands of your best citizens

(and the worst), for I am in close relationship with the Angel of Death."

Three more attacks occurred in August, September, and October 1919, the only ones to have come after the letter was released by the press. No-one died in those attacks but the victims were left scarred for life. They were the last to be directly associated with the Axeman.

Allegedly, the Axeman vanished from New Orleans in 1919 and was never seen again but modern research has a new take on the killings, along with the suggestion there was no Axeman at all.

Researchers scouring the doldrums of newspaper archives discovered murders that took place in 1920 and 1921 in other cities in Louisiana, that were said to be remarkably similar to the Axeman murders of New Orleans. It led to a suspicion the Axeman had left the city only to take up killing elsewhere.

The method and process were the same as the New Orleans killings. Joseph Spero and his daughter were killed in Alexandria in December 1920, Giovanni Orlando in Deridder in January 1921, and Frank Scalisi in Lake Charles in April 1921. All of them were Italian grocers who were attacked with an axe in the middle of the night.

Other researchers have found similar murders as early as 1910.

One of the more curious theories was that the Axeman was angered by the U.S. Navy shutting down the red-light district which included brothels, gambling dens, and dance halls where jazz was allowed to flourish. But it didn't explain why Italians were targeted.

In a book by Miriam Davis published in 2017, it is claimed the letter to the paper was not written by the Axeman at all. The author suggested the Axeman was not well-educated and was probably a burglar but the person who wrote the letter was well-educated and well-versed. But this doesn't explain why no money or items were stolen from the crime scenes.

It is suggested that jazz composer John Joseph Davila wrote the letter, because right after the letter was published, he released a composition called *'The Mysterious Axeman's Jazz (Don't Scare Me Papa).'* Or maybe the press at the time – who were known for fantastical exaggeration – created the letter for impact and Davila cashed in on it.

Black Hand extortion remains the most likely scenario where blackmailing gangs extorted the better-off Italian businesses for protection money, then made an example of them when they refused to pay. It would mean the murders would have been carried out by multiple people, in a city rife with crime.

Murders that were associated with the Axeman in other locations at different times could have been the work of copycat killers, perpetuating the unsolved mystery of the Axeman of New Orleans.

The suspect or suspects in the Axeman killings have never been identified and the murders remain unsolved to this day, confined to a moment in New Orleans history when jazz and racial tension were on the rise. The Axeman, however, did have one last thing to say in his letter.

"Well, as I am cold and crave the warmth of my native Tartarus, and it is about time I leave your earthly home, I will cease my discourse. Hoping that thou wilt publish this, that it may go well with thee, I have been, am and will be the worst spirit that ever existed either in fact or realm of fancy."

The Norfolk Woods Butcher

In the Norfolk woods, a man was found butchered to death, believed to have been mauled by a wild beast, but he was the victim of a former Marine with a hatred for dog walkers.

Harling is a small civil parish in the Breckland district Norfolk, with a population of a little over 2,000. The village of East Harling is the principal settlement within the parish, a few miles northeast of Thetford.

The picturesque village is situated on the gentle sloping southern side of the valley of the River Thet, and it can date its heritage back to the 11th Century, where it was mentioned in two wills uncovered by local historians.

Modern researchers, who form the backbone of future history, will now forever connect the village of East Harling with cold-blooded murder. On 5th August 2017, 83-year-old local dog walker Peter Wrighton, was out walking his dog on the heath when he was attacked from behind.

The attacker, who crept up on Peter, was 24-year-old former Royal Marine Alexander Palmer. Peter had no chance, as Palmer stabbed him in the back, pushed him to the ground and stabbed him a total of 45 times, before dumping his body under brambles on the heath.

When Peter didn't return home, his family contacted police. Later that day, walkers found his body on the heath. The initial investigation were convinced that Peter had been mauled by a wild beast, as the wounds to his body were severe.

So brutal in fact, that his head had almost been severed from the rest of his body. When the body was taken for examination, it was concluded that Peter had not been mauled by an animal, but by a man with a knife.

Commando

A large murder investigation began but police hit a stumbling block immediately as there was no obvious motive behind the murder. Peter was a well-liked retired BT engineer, who lived in the village with his wife of 59 years.

That an 83-year-old man of slight build was murdered in such a fashion sent shockwaves across Norfolk and the country, for nothing like it had ever been seen in the area. Unknown to police at the time, the murder itself could have been stopped before it happened.

Palmer was a teenager when he signed up for the Royal Marine Commandos in 2010, served with 29 Commando, and was based at RAF Marham. He had a promising future with the Marines and wanted to continue a career with them.

In late 2014, he was violently attacked by a fellow trainee commando. The attack left his head crushed in such a way that it began to affect his cognitive ability. By 2015, Palmer was discharged for medical reasons, relating to mental health.

When he returned home, his family were met with a different person, as the attack had changed his mannerisms and behaviour. To help him through civilian life and the result of the attack, he was seen by multiple mental health professionals.

In late 2015, Palmer was sectioned under the Mental Health Act and admitted to a psychiatric hospital in Peterborough. He told professionals there that he wanted to get rid of people on the street, especially dog walkers, by stringing them up and cutting them open.

Wanting to be a serial killer

He was discharged in early 2016 and put under community mental health care which ended shortly after. Palmer's parents became concerned when he started buying knives and began talking of killing people.

Unsure if he was being sincere in his conversations, they wrote letters to mental health professionals and his GP, asking for an intervention. There were two psychiatric reports stating that Palmer was going to kill somebody, how he was going to do it, and that it was inevitable.

But the letters went unheard, as the professionals suggested his parents were busybodies, interfering in his mental health care. At the trial, the court learned there had been multiple letters and notes between mental health professionals over a two-year period before the murder, all of which documented Palmer's violent fantasies.

He also claimed to hear voices in his head, and that he had developed the plan to kill dog walkers. He even pre-empted the murder by saying he wanted to be a serial killer. He told one mental health professional that '*he would be on a pedestal, up with the big ones, everyone would look up to me, everyone would know me by name.*' All of it was ignored.

On that fateful morning, Palmer drove to the heath with the intention of butchering another human being. He waited behind the treeline for the next person to walk along the heath, which just so happened to be Peter, then crept up behind him and slaughtered him.

He drove home afterwards and seemed happy with what he had done. Less than two hours after the murder, he took a selfie in his home, with a family member in the background. Police later found the phone with the selfie on, as if Palmer had been documenting the murder.

Little Alex

Despite the difficulty in uncovering a motive, the investigation into the murder moved along quickly. When police reached out for information, they were contacted by a military psychologist, who suggested they look at Palmer, after she had treated him at RAF Marham.

She claimed that Palmer had a voice in his head called 'Little Alex' who told him to stab dog walkers in the throat. It wasn't a coincidence that Peter had been stabbed nine times in the neck. She gave police Palmer's number plate, which was L666AHP.

Using traffic highway cameras, police tracked the car on the morning of the attack to the area of the murder scene. Realising they may had found the killer, police swooped in on Palmer's family home and arrested him a few days after the murder.

Palmer was taken in for questioning, and when asked if the car was his, he confirmed that his mother bought it for him for his birthday. He then laughed when the number plate was read out and said, *'I'm a little devil.'*

A police officer interviewing Palmer asked him if that was a joke, and Palmer agreed, sniggering as he did so. He denied murdering Peter but the evidence against him was growing. The prosecution were already building a strong case, including DNA evidence that was found at the scene of the murder.

Allowed to kill

On 28th February 2018, it took just 44 minutes to find Palmer guilty of murder. Despite suffering a psychotic disorder, Palmer was sentenced to life in prison with a minimum term of 28 years. Due to the severity of the murder, Palmer was sent to Wakefield Prison, the notorious Monster Mansion, to serve out his sentence.

The story of Palmer carried on for many years afterwards, as the mental health professionals who treated him were subjected to public and professional scrutiny. Peter's family learned that Palmer was discharged from community mental health care with a text message and wasn't given any anti-psychotic medication.

Palmer was seen by dozens of different mental health professionals, which is common, but means there was dilution when diagnosing him. Peter's family helped with a campaign to see mental health systems improved, including reducing the number of people involved in a patient's care.

Though they did not excuse Palmer for his actions, there were opportunities for mental health professionals and doctors to have stopped him before he killed. With the right attention to care, Palmer could have come out the other side a better human being. Instead, he chose to kill.

For many years, mental health care in the UK has been underfunded and understaffed, so its perhaps no surprise the system was being set up to fail. The commando who viciously attacked Palmer, who some say caused his mental health problems, has never been held to account.

However, there is only so much one can do to help someone who is adamant on committing evil. Palmer had created in his head a dark fantasy of becoming a serial killer, and it appeared no one was going to stop him murdering another human being.

He was not tried as someone suffering from mental disability, which meant he was fully cognitive and able at the time of the murder. During the trial, reports from various mental health quarters were heard, and despite his fantasy, Palmer stood trial as a person in control of their actions.

What he did to Peter Wrighton was as abnormal as it got, but Palmer killed because he wanted to become a serial killer, to fulfil the fantasy he had given himself. Had he not been stopped after the one murder, then it's likely he would have gone on to kill again – and again.

Maniac Cop

In one of modern times most eerie unsolved cold cases, a fitness instructor was killed in a local church by a person dressed in police SWAT gear.

Terri 'Missy' Bevers was no stranger to exercise, she had spent most of her adult life teaching others the benefits of a full body workout. Just before 4am on 18th April 2016, Missy left her home in Red Oak, Texas, and drove to the Creekside Church of Christ in Midlothian, 19 miles away.

She arrived at the church at 4.20am in the pouring rain and began setting up one of the rooms for her early morning Camp Gladiator class, which normally kicked off at 5am. Little did Missy know but someone else was already in the church waiting for her.

Just before 5am, the boot camp students began arriving. When they entered the room where the class was taking place, they found Missy lying on her back having been beaten and bludgeoned multiple times.

In a panic, the students called 911 and paramedics rushed to the church but it was too late as Missy was pronounced dead at the scene. When detectives arrived on scene, it was clear that Missy had been murdered, and the first suspicion was a robbery gone wrong.

When the church owners checked the building and its belongings, it appeared that nothing had been stolen, and Missy was still wearing her wedding ring. When investigators checked the CCTV from inside the church, they were shocked by what they saw.

Full tactical gear

Prior to retrieving the security footage, a search of the building revealed that many windows were broken and that the main door had been smashed through, meaning that Missy's murderer was already in the building when she arrived.

When police sat down to review the footage, the suspect was revealed. At 3.50am, footage showed a person wearing full police tactical or SWAT gear breaking into the church. The suspected burglar, who was masked in a full black helmet, began wandering the church.

The footage is eerie, as the person slowly and calmly wanders the dark hallways of the building, casually opening doors and occasionally smashing windows with the hammer they have in their hand. The person was estimated at being between 5'2" and 5'7" but the sex of the person could not be ascertained.

Whether the person inside the suit was male or female, they had an unusual gait which caused them to limp with their feet pointed slightly outwards. At 4.20am, Missy is seen entering the church and making her way to her classroom, unaware of the mysterious person traipsing through the building.

Within a few minutes of arriving in the darkened classroom, Missy was assaulted and beaten to death. Further CCTV footage showed a 2010-2012 Nissan Altima or Infiniti G37 stopping at a car park near to the church in the hours before the attack. The car didn't stay long but the owner has never been identified.

Witnesses saw a dark-coloured SUV driving from the church around 4.30am but the driver has also never been identified. Either one of the drivers of the vehicles could have been the killer. In the weeks that followed, police focused their attention on Missy's husband.

Suspects

Brandon Bevers had been having troubles in his marriage to Missy due to ongoing financial issues and cracks in their relationship. Police revealed they were talking to Brandon in relation to the case which caused the press and social media users to blame him.

But after a year-long investigation, police concluded that Brandon was not involved in his wife's death, and he was on a fishing trip in California at the time. Police stated that no member of her direct or indirect family were responsible, which began to raise questions. Most importantly, who had killed Missy?

Before they cleared the Bevers family of any wrongdoing, Brandon's father had taken a blood-soaked shirt to a dry cleaners in the days following the murder. He claimed he had broken up a dog fight, and the blood tests on the shirt confirmed he was telling the truth. There's not many killers dumb enough to take a bloody shirt to the dry cleaners, but police were looking everywhere.

Missy was active on the business social network LinkedIn, and when investigators went through her devices and accounts, they found she was talking to a man for three months before her murder, and that the messages were flirtatious in nature.

The man was interviewed and admitted to a friendship but was ruled out as a suspect due to his location and an alibi on the night of the murder. However, Missy had told friends in the days before her murder that she was receiving creepy and strange messages from a man she didn't know.

The final message was sent three days before the murder but police have never released the details of the message and it remains unclear if the sender was a suspect or just someone who was an annoyance to Missy.

Based on the SUV tip, investigators were led to former police officer Bobby Wayne Henry as a suspect as he owned a dark coloured SUV and still had his police tactical gear despite being fired in 2017 for sexual assault and possession of child pornography.

Despite the links, Bobby was several inches taller than the person in the CCTV footage which immediately ruled him out. Since 2017, the Missy murder case has fallen into the realm of the unsolved but it hasn't stopped investigators and web sleuths taking hold of the reigns.

Effective disguise

The tactical police gear disguise was so effective that no analysts could confirm without a shadow of a doubt if the person was male or female, though there were leaning more on the side of male due to the gait and the fact they killed with a hammer. Female killers rarely use objects that require strength, preferring methods such as poison.

Many still believe it was a robbery gone wrong but with no effort to take anything, the theory doesn't hold up. On the CCTV footage, the killer opens various doors without entering and passes by many others they don't bother to check, as if they are looking for something – or someone – specifically.

The casual walk of the person goes against every burglar/robber stereotype, who generally move quickly to get hold of their loot and get out before they're noticed, which makes the CCTV footage all that eerier. None of their actions make them out to be a burglar.

One theory points towards a teenage vandal as some of the inner windows were smashed but the person walks past many opportunities to vandalise and doesn't. And again, the casualness of the person's movements don't match someone who is intent on vandalising.

It most likely meant that Missy was the target of the killer and had been deliberately chosen by someone who knew she would be there alone. Due to her being known for fitness classes and her affinity for LinkedIn and Facebook, where she would share many details of her life, there is the possibility she may have had a stalker, which could have been the person who sent the creepy messages.

Maniac cop

Due to her fitness instructor career, she met many random members of the public which suggests she may have known her killer. The killer could have had their sexual advances rejected which led to them wanting to kill Missy so no one else could have her. But it remains only a theory.

It is unusual that the case has never been solved, due to its very clear security footage, witness statements regarding vehicles, and the names and locations of all Missy's students. But it is the SWAT gear that sets the murder aside from any other.

There would have been plenty of ways to disguise oneself when committing a crime and full police tactical gear is not the usual one. If the killer was attempting to confuse the investigation while hiding their identity, then it worked.

Some researchers have suggested the killer was a female due to the way they were holding the hammer on the footage. That the killer was overweight, as seen by the fit of the uniform and their gait, suggests that maybe they were someone who Missy had either embarrassed or ridiculed. Maybe they were waiting for Missy, to enact their revenge.

Who killed Missy and why remains a mystery to this day. It is unusual and creepy that there is so much evidence to go on and so little progress. The so-called maniac cop seems to have got away with murder, and if they are never caught in this life, then they will be judged in the next.

Babes in the Wood 1986

Two nine-year-old girls were lured to their deaths by a monster who escaped justice for 32 years due to errors in the way forensics handled the original evidence.

The moniker of Babes in the Wood refers to four separate incidents across Britain, Canada, and the United States. The first, known as the Pine Grove Furnace murders was in Pennsylvania, where in 1934, the bodies of three young girls were found under a blanket in the woods. They were killed by their father who shot himself the next day.

The next was in Vancouver, Canada, in 1953, where the remains of two male children were found in a shallow grave in remote woodland. In early 2022, they were identified as Derek and

David D'Alton, who had been killed in 1947 by an unknown murderer.

The first Babes in the Wood murders in Britain happened in 1970, when 11-year-old Susan Muriel Blatchford and 12-year-old Gary John Hanlon were raped and murdered by Ronald Jebson. He left their bodies in open woodland near Sewardstone, Essex.

Jebson was already serving a life sentence for the murder of another girl in 1974 when he confessed to the Blatchford/Hanlon murders and was sentenced to additional life terms. He died in 2015 and if he hadn't confessed, the murders may not have ever been solved.

The Babes in the Wood murders in this story are perhaps the most infamous and were the ones directly named after the children's tale of the same name. In the 16th Century English children's tale, two children are abandoned in a wood, who then die and are covered with leaves by birds.

On 9th October 1986, two nine-year-old girls, Nicola Fellows and Karen Hadaway, were lured to their deaths by then 20-year-old local roofing contractor, Russell Bishop. But the double murder case which haunted the city, remained unsolved for 32 years.

Last time seen alive

Brighton is one of the largest cities on the South Coast of England, approximately 50 miles south of London, and sometimes known as London-by-the-Sea. It's been home to its fair share of infamous crimes and murders but perhaps none more so than the Babes in the Wood double murder.

Nicola and Karen were school friends who played outside a lot and spent most of their free time together. The best friends lived close to each other in the Brighton suburb of Moulsecoomb, just north of the busier parts of the city.

On Thursday 9th October 1986, they both went home after school before getting changed into their play clothes and meeting each other outside. At around 5pm, just an hour before the girls were due to go home for dinner, Nicola's mother, Susan, saw her daughter and Karen playing with their roller skates.

It was the last time that Susan would see her daughter alive. About an hour later at 6pm, a 14-year-old neighbour saw the girls near shops in Lewes Road and told them to go home as it was getting late and their parents would be worried.

The girls ignored the 14-year-old, and Nicola was heard saying to Karen that they should go to the local nature reserve of Wild Park, a location they were not allowed to go to by themselves, due to the size of the park, and the possibility of them getting lost in the woods.

Half hour later, at 6.30pm, the girls were still in Lewes Road, beside a police telephone box, but their killer, Russell Bishop, was seen loitering near them. It was the last time the girls were ever seen alive, except by Bishop, who lured them to their deaths.

Wild Park

When dinnertime in the Fellows and Hadaway households had come and gone, the families began to panic. Susan called Karen's mother, Michelle, to find out what had happened but both families were in the dark as they both thought the girls would be at their friend's homes.

In the early evening, Michelle called the police and the girls disappearances were taken seriously, as it was completely out of character for them. As the night darkened, a 200-strong search party was put together involving police and residents of Moulsecoomb.

Bishop joined the search with his dog but deliberately searched in the wrong areas, trying to hide the fact he knew where the girls were. However, as the search went into the following morning, and then the afternoon, the search team at Wild Park were getting closer and Bishop found himself moving closer to the girls.

In the early afternoon of the 10th, two searchers and residents of Moulsecoomb, Kevin Rowland and Matthew Marchant, came across a makeshift den in the woods. They looked inside and found the bodies of Nicola and Karen, lying side by side. They had been raped and strangled to death.

Despite looking in different locations, when Bishop caught wind that the search team was close to the den, he moved towards it with a purpose. When Rowland and Marchant found the bodies, Bishop ran towards the den with a police officer.

Bishop claimed that he touched the girl's necks to check for a pulse. However, the police officer closest to Bishop at the time the bodies were found, stated that Bishop was too far away to have touched the girls. It was the first of many inconsistencies in Bishop's story that would lead to his arrest.

Bodged prosecution

Bishop told police that he was in Moulsecoomb the evening of the girl's disappearances as he intended to steal a car, which was an odd thing to have admitted to police. He then told other search party members that he had gone to a newsagent to buy a newspaper but realised he had no money and went home.

When interviewed by detectives, he told a different story, and said that he was going to visit his teenage girlfriend but didn't show up as he had got high on cannabis and went home instead. Bishop became one of the prime suspects in the case but the police had worryingly little evidence to go on, despite it being public knowledge that Bishop took a liking to young teenage girls.

His claim of touching the girls necks upon their discovery meant he would have left fingerprint evidence, something that would help in his case, despite the officer claiming he was nowhere near. Still, with all the other inconsistencies, Bishop was arrested on Halloween of the same year and charged with both murders.

His trial, over a year later in December 1987, would prove to be one of the greatest miscarriages of justice Brighton had ever seen, and it was all down to a bodged prosecution, in which a series of errors were made.

Firstly, the pathologist and forensic team failed to take the temperature of the bodies and could not accurately give a time of death, which played havoc with witness statements. The prosecution merely suggested the girls had been killed between 5.15pm and 6.30pm but could not back it up with forensic evidence.

It meant that all of Bishop's alibis could not be argued as he claimed to have been away from Lewes Road and Wild Park by that time. With no witness statements seeing him beyond 6.15pm, they couldn't conclusively prove that Bishop was in Wild Park, and the blunders didn't stop there.

Biggest flaws

Further forensic mistakes helped bolster Bishop's defence that he wasn't the killer. Despite both girls being strangled to death, the hand marks around their necks were never measured and fingerprints were never lifted at the scene, only later at the autopsies, which by that point, there were numerous fingerprints, including Bishop's.

Forensic experts also failed to analyse blood that was discovered on Karen's underwear, which may have helped convict the killer. The prosecution then tried to push a blue sweatshirt as a key piece of evidence.

The sweatshirt, they believed Bishop was wearing at the time of the murders, was found discarded near a railway track in Moulsecoomb. Police had a written statement from Bishop's girlfriend, Jennifer Johnson, in that she claimed the sweatshirt belonged to Bishop. With Bishop denying the sweatshirt belonged to him, the prosecution thought they had a damning testimony that proved he was lying.

When Johnson took the stand, she denied having ever seen the sweatshirt before, and gave testimony that she had never mentioned the sweatshirt in the statement, and that it had been fabricated by police and her signature forged, in order for the police to secure a conviction.

But the biggest flaw in the prosecution's case was the time of death, because they simply didn't have one, at least not backed up by scientific evidence. The judge in the trial told the jury that unless they were sure the girls were dead by 6.30pm then they should acquit Bishop.

However, there were witness statements that put the girls and Bishop in Lewes Road at 6.30pm which meant the girls were not killed before 6.30pm, meaning the jury's hand was forced. Bishop was acquitted of both the rapes and murders of both girls and went on to sell his story as a wrongfully accused man to The News of the World newspaper for £15,000.

Devil's Dyke attack

The acquittal meant that the double murder case remained open and the investigation looked elsewhere for their suspects. It materialised afterwards that Bishop had gone to Nicola's house the afternoon of their disappearance to talk to his friend, Dougie Judd, who was a lodger who lived there but Nicola had told him to go away.

In The News of the World article, both Bishop and his girlfriend accused a family member from one of the girl's families of being involved. They believed that Barrie Fellows, Nicola's father, was guilty and that they had been set up by police as they were under pressure to find a suspect.

As the Babes in the Wood murders fell under the banner of the coldest of the cold, investigators looked at all possibilities. Bishop's friend, Dougie, and Barrie Fellows were arrested for the murders at various points over the years but there was no evidence linking them, aside from circumstantial.

Four years after the murders, in 1990, a seven-year-old girl was kidnapped and raped at Devil's Dyke in Brighton. She was strangled and left for dead but went on to survive the attack and point out her attacker to police; it was none other than Bishop.

He was found guilty of the attack and sentenced to life in prison with a minimum term of 14 years but at both parole hearings, he was denied release, and 32 years later, would be found guilty of the murders of Nicola and Karen. And it all happened because of a change in the law, specifically relating to the double-jeopardy rule.

Advancements in DNA technology

A new ruling in 2005, changed the double-jeopardy rule which meant a suspect could face a new trial if substantial new evidence came to light. But in 2006, the courts decided there was not enough new evidence to charge Bishop in a second trial for the murders.

In 2012, a new forensics team were given access to the evidence in the case, re-examined it, and discovered DNA evidence. They proved that the sweatshirt did belong to Bishop and found traces of his DNA on material taken from Karen's body.

Bishop was arrested while in prison in 2016 and charged with the murders, 30 years after the fact. A year later, an appeals court removed the acquittals from the 1987 trial which meant that Bishop could be charged at a second trial.

In December 2018, Bishop was found guilty of the murders of Nicola and Karen and sentenced to two additional life sentences with a minimum tariff of 36 years. The trial was only possible because of advancements in DNA technology, and that evidence from the case had been so well stored.

In May 2021, Bishop's ex-girlfriend, Jennifer Johnson, was found guilty of perjury after she admitted lying about Bishop's ownership of the sweatshirt. She was sentenced to six years in prison. On 20th January 2022, Bishop was rushed to hospital where he died of complications with cancer.

The Babes in the Wood case goes to show how entire trials can go either way on the smallest pieces of evidence. Had Jennifer confirmed the sweatshirt belonged to Bishop, and had forensics done their jobs properly, then Bishop would have been convicted sooner, meaning he wouldn't have been free to attack the seven-year-old girl in 1990.

Though there are a number of murders given the moniker of Babes in the Wood, there is none more heinous and infamous than the Brighton murders, of two innocent friends playing with each other in the park, only to have their innocence and lives ripped away by a monster.

Murder of Marvin Gaye

Marvin Gaye helped shape Motown in the 1960s and went on to become one of the most influential American artists of all time – who was shot dead by his own cross-dressing preacher father.

Marvin Gaye is perhaps one of the most influential American artists of all time and helped shape the sound of Motown from the 1960s onwards. His accolades include inductions into the 'Rhythm and Blues Music Hall of Fame', the 'Songwriters Hall of Fame', and the 'Rock and Roll Hall of Fame.'

Though his voice is still heard across the world, and his work continues to influence people to this day, many may not remember or even know that Gaye was shot dead by his own father following an argument in 1984.

It was a murder that sent ripples throughout the world of soul music and beyond, his death comparable with that of John Lennon and Elvis Presley, who were all featured on first class postage stamps for the Postal Service's Music Icons series.

It remains a point of sadness and bizarreness that Gaye's last words insinuated that he had wanted his father to kill him, telling his brother Frankie, '*I got what I wanted. I couldn't do it myself, so I made him do it.*'

Here, we take a deep dive into the bizarre death of Marvin Gaye and the events leading up to it, including abuse at the hands of his own father, theories of a planned suicide, and the loss of a legend known as The Prince of Motown. For the purposes of this story, Marvin Gaye is referred to as Gaye, and his father, Marvin Gay Sr., referred to as Marvin.

Born Marvin Gay Jr. in 1939, Washington, D.C., he added an 'e' to the end of his name to stop himself being bullied at school but his school life was the least of his worries. His home was where the true evil remained hidden from sight.

His father ran his home like a prison who frequently beat his son, starved his children and abused his wife, Alberta Cooper, in front of them.

Marvin had already shown his dark side when he married the then 20-year-old Alberta.

She had a child by another man before they met but Marvin refused to bring up another man's child so he ordered her to send the baby away to live with her sister. When Gaye was born, Marvin took an instant dislike to him, believing that he wasn't really his child.

He refused to love Gaye in the way he would his other children and convinced Alberta that she should show less love to him. Despite his abuse, violent behaviour, and psychological torture, Marvin was a man of God.

He was a preacher at the Hebrew Pentecostal Church in Washington, D.C., and part of the church known as the House of God which advocated strict conduct and banned make-up, films, and TV.

Marvin was also an alcoholic and known womaniser who was later found to have had affairs behind Alberta's back and even had a child with another woman, despite his hatred against Alberta's first child, born before she had even met him. But his hypocrisy didn't stop there.

Gaye later described living in his father's house as '*living with a king, a very peculiar, changeable, cruel, and all-powerful king.*' Marvin forced them to quote bible verses from memory, with any mistakes punishable by severe beatings and whippings.

Marvin was known to enjoy wearing women's clothes and shoes and would sometimes deliver a hard whipping to Gaye while dressed as a woman. In response to starving his children, he claimed that their hunger would bring them closer to God.

According to his siblings, Gaye received the worst of the beatings and punishments, mostly because Marvin believed he was not his son. He would abuse Alberta whenever she gave attention to Gaye and went as far as accusing them of sleeping together – which they weren't.

Yet, it was Alberta who supported her son's talent in singing, while Marvin refused at every step of the way to back his son's endeavours. Gaye said in a later interview that if it wasn't for his mother, he would have taken his own life before he was a teenager, such was the brutality and hatred he received at the hands of his father.

Gaye achieved early success with *The Marquees*, who were a four-piece doo-wop band, founded in 1957 and operating out of Washington D.C. Other notable members included Bo Diddley, Billy Stewart, and Harvey Fuqua; the uncle of American filmmaker Antoine Fuqua.

Gaye moved with Fuqua to Detroit where he began a career as a solo artist. Within a decade, he was one of the biggest selling living artists on the planet, with the 1968 single 'I Heard it Through the Grapevine' going on to sell four-million copies.

And despite the rise to extraordinary fame, Marvin still hated his son and they never found any peace going forward. He despised his son's foray into the entertainment industry and resented him even more when he began making more money than him.

After a battle with alcoholism and cocaine abuse, Gaye returned to the big time in 1983 during the sold out *Sexual Healing Tour*. But the success of the tour led Gaye back to cocaine and into a veil of paranoia, instigated by the childhood abuse he had received from his father.

In August of 1983, he returned to his parent's home, a mansion he had purchased for them a decade earlier in Los Angeles, California, to look after his mother who was recovering from kidney surgery. His father returned to the home after a lengthy business trip in October that year, and for the next six months, Gaye and Marvin argued daily.

By late 1983, Gaye had become suicidal due to paranoia that someone was out to kill him and that he was being followed by stalkers, no doubt backed up by cocaine over-use, and a father who still ruled over him like a king. He was known to perform on stage wearing a bullet-proof vest.

In the days leading up to the murder, his parents argued to the point of Marvin becoming aggressive towards Alberta. Gaye stood up to his father and ordered him to leave his mother alone. Not liking being shouted at by his son, Marvin simmered through the night.

On 1st April 1984, shortly after noon, Marvin continued an argument about an insurance document that had cut him out. Gaye then pushed him out of his bedroom and began beating him up, throwing punches to the face and kicking him in the torso.

Alberta begged him to stop because Marvin had once told her if any one of his children laid a hand on him out of violence, that he would take up his God-given right to murder that child. Gaye left his badly-beaten father outside his own bedroom.

Minutes later, Marvin staggered to Gaye's bedroom, with a pistol that Gaye had given him for Christmas. He remained silent as he shot his son two times. The first bullet hit Gaye in the shoulder, and as he fell down, Marvin stood over him and shot him in the heart.

Gaye's brother, Frankie, was living in a guesthouse in the grounds of the mansion, when he heard the shots. He charged into the house and found Alberta screaming for help, before running up the stairs to Gaye's bedroom.

Frankie held his brother in his arms and heard his last words, which were, *'I got what I wanted. I couldn't do it myself, so I had him do it. It's good, I ran my race, there's no more left in me.'*

Police arrived within minutes and arrested Marvin who was sitting on the step of the front porch. They later found the gun under his pillow. Gaye was rushed to hospital but was dead on arrival, just one day before his 45th birthday.

The autopsy showed there were traces of cocaine and PCP in Gaye's system. PCP is known to sometimes cause the user to become violent and may have been one of the many reasons why Gaye was finally able to stand up to his father, albeit in a violent manner.

Marvin told the police he was scared of his son and kept the gun nearby in case he was attacked, which was allegedly something he feared. He also claimed he didn't know there were any bullets in the gun and had fired the weapon in self-defence.

He was held at a Los Angeles jail as the case was built against him. After having a tumour removed from the base of his brain, psychiatrists interviewed him to ascertain whether he was fit to stand trial. When they found him competent, the investigation got underway.

In July 1984, Alberta filed for divorce, citing Gaye's death as the last straw of a violent relationship. Marvin's defence team filed a plea deal for a voluntary manslaughter charge, which was agreed by the judge due to the amount of drugs in Gaye's system and the injuries Gaye had inflicted on his father.

Marvin was convicted and given a six-year suspended sentence along with five years of probation. During the sentencing, Marvin claimed to have loved his son and reiterated that it was self-defence, believing Gaye could have killed him in the attack.

As the death had happened on April Fool's Day, many of Gaye's fellow artists and fans assumed news of his death to be a joke. As the world began to realise that Marvin Gaye had really been killed, there was an outpouring of grief, in what was referred to as a dark day in music.

In an unusual twist, Gaye's siblings believed his death to be a pre-meditated suicide. They claimed Gaye knew that by attacking his father, he would murder him as he'd always promised. That way, he could die without actually killing himself, which is what he wanted, and get his father taken away from his mother at the same time.

To this day, Gaye's siblings and friends are confident he had instigated his own death. By having his father carry out the act, it was the ultimate punishment Gaye could bestow upon him, knowing he would be haunted until the end of his days. Marvin died of natural causes in October 1998, aged 84.

In 1987, shortly after founding the Marvin P. Gaye Jr. Memorial Foundation, to help those suffering from drug abuse and alcoholism, Alberta died of bone cancer, knowing her son's legacy would inspire, help, and influence future generations.

Marvin Gaye's death shocks to this day and tributes are still paid to him across the world, through songs, music, and film. Like other music greats, his name rose above the bizarre circumstances of his death and moved into legend – as The Prince of Motown.

As a thank you for adding this book to your collection, we would like to offer you a FREE eBook for simply signing up to our mailing list. Along with a free book, you'll get weekly updates from the world of true crime brought to you by truecrimelists.com, and early book release notifications so you can be the first to get them at an introductory price, exclusively for subscribers.

Visit WWW.TRUECRIMELISTS.COM and click on FREE BOOK from the menu.

www.ingramcontent.com/pod-product-compliance
Lightning Source LLC
LaVergne TN
LVHW051116080426
835510LV00018B/2073